The Tofu Cookbook

The Tofu Cookbook

HIGH-PROTEIN • LOW-FAT • LOW-CHOLESTEROL • 80 RECIPES

BECKY JOHNSON

LORENZ BOOKS

This edition is published by Lorenz Books,
an imprint of Anness Publishing Ltd,
108 Great Russell Street, London WC1B 3NA
info@anness.com

www.lorenzbooks.com; www.annesspublishing.com;
twitter:@Anness_Books

Publisher: Joanna Lorenz
Special photography: William Shaw
Food for special photography: Heather Whinney
Designer: Nigel Partridge
Jacket designer: Adelle Mahoney
Editorial: Helen Sudell
Recipes: Catherine Atkinson, Ghillie Basan, Judy Bastyra,
Matthew Drennen, Yasuko Fukuoka, Nicola Graimes, Kathy
Man, Sallie Morris, Deh-Ta Hsuing, Terry Tan
Photographers: Tim Auty, Martin Brigdale, Nicky Dowey,
Michelle Garrett, Amanda Heywood, Janine Hosegood,
William Lingwood, Tom Odulate, Craig Robertson.
Production controller: Ben Worley

COOK'S NOTES
Bracketed terms are intended for American readers.
For all recipes, quantities are given in both metric and imperial
measures and, where appropriate, in standard cups and
spoons. Follow one set of measures, but not a mixture, because
they are not interchangeable.
Standard spoon and cup measures are level.
1 tsp = 5ml, 1 tbsp = 15ml, 1 cup = 250ml/8fl oz.
Australian standard tablespoons are 20ml. Australian readers
should use 3 tsp in place of 1 tbsp for measuring small
quantities. American pints are 16fl oz/2 cups. American readers
should use 20fl oz/2.5 cups in place of 1 pint when measuring
liquids.
Electric oven temperatures in this book are for conventional
ovens. When using a fan oven, the temperature will probably
need to be reduced by about 10–20°C/20–40°F. Since ovens
vary, you should check with your manufacturer's instruction
book for guidance.
The nutritional analysis given for each recipe is calculated per
portion (i.e. serving or item), unless otherwise stated. If the
recipe gives a range, such as Serves 4–6, then the nutritional
analysis will be for the smaller portion size, i.e. 6 servings.
The analysis does not include optional ingredients, such as salt
added to taste.

Contents

Introduction

Above: The soy bean (*Glycine max*) came originally from Asia but is now grown around the world. It is one of the few plants that contains all eight amino acids that are essential for human health.

Right: The subtle flavour and soft texture of tofu means that it works well in all kinds of ingredients.

Although it is best known in the West by its Japanese name, tofu actually originated in China around 200 BCE and was not introduced to Japan until the 8th century AD. Soya beans have been cultivated in China for thousands of years and many by-products from this valuable legume still constitute an important part of the Chinese diet. However, exactly how cooks developed the technique for making tofu, or bean curd as it is also known, is lost in the mists of the past.

Tofu was originally the food of Chinese aristocrats, noblemen and monks – indeed, it was Buddhist priests who first took Mongolian doufu to Japan during the Tang dynasty. Eating it was thought to promote longevity, a much-prized virtue in traditional Chinese philosophy, and these elite classes certainly did live the longest. By the 16th century, the population at large had adopted tofu into their diet and by the late 1700s, tofu cookbooks, extolling the benefits of the humble bean curd, had become increasingly popular.

Different types of tofu – from cotton-strained and silken to fermented and marinated – have been developed over the centuries. The Japanese were quick to create more refined forms of tofu, as well as inventing other soya products that matched the subtlety and delicacy of their cuisine. In China and Japan today, tofu is one of the most commonly used cooking ingredients and is held in high regard due to its culinary flexibility and nutritional value.

Until the 20th century tofu had only been sampled by Westerners who had travelled to China and Japan. It remained a foreign curiosity until the early 1900s when the methods and techniques for tofu manufacture were introduced into Europe. From then on, tofu was made and used in the West. As the numbers of vegetarians and vegans increased, tofu, in all its forms, became more widely available, migrating from a few specialist health-food stores to many mainstream supermarkets. Modern medical concerns about cholesterol levels, obesity and dietary links with illnesses such as cancers and heart disease, have stimulated people to seek healthier foodstuffs. Tofu contains isoflavones which are thought to lower cholesterol levels and more and more people are becoming aware of its other health benefits as well as its great versatility in cooking.

Above: Firm tofu (left), marinated tofu (centre), and silken tofu (right) are the most common types of tofu available.

Opposite, top: Firm tofu can be sliced, chopped into cubes, and processed or marinated prior to cooking.

Opposite, bottom right: It is easy to boost protein in your diet by adding spoonfuls of soya powder or soya milk in place of dairy milk.

MAKING TOFU

The process of making tofu is a relatively straightforward process. It is a little like making soft cheese but much less time-consuming. Soya beans are soaked, boiled, mashed and then sieved to produce soya 'milk'. Curds are then produced with the addition of a coagulant and, while warm, these are set in moulds for several hours. Finally, the tofu is released into a water tank to firm and cool further. The curds are processed differently depending on the form of tofu that is being made. For the standard firm tofu, the curd is cut and strained of excess liquid using cheesecloth or muslin, and then lightly pressed to produce a soft cake. If a firmer tofu is required then the tofu is further pressed to remove even more liquid. Soft silken tofu is made from thicker soya milk and isn't pressed at all, instead the soya milk is curdled directly in the tofu's packaging.

NUTRITION

Tofu and the closely related Indonesian tempeh are just two of the products that are made from the highly nutritious soya bean. Soya beans contain all eight amino acids that are required to produce a complete protein that is so essential for our body's health. Furthermore, because the manufacturing process removes the less digestible parts of the beans, our bodies can absorb 95 per cent of the protein present in tofu. Consequently, it is a good food for young babies, the elderly and convalescents, as well as for vegetarians and vegans. In its raw state, tofu is gluten free, although some marinated tofu may contain gluten. Tofu is extremely low in carbohydrates and is cholesterol-free.

Tofu is also rich in vitamins and minerals. It is an excellent source of iron and the minerals manganese, selenium and phosphorous. In addition, it is a good source of magnesium, zinc, copper and vitamin B1.

Tofu and soya bean products are high in linoleic acid, an unsaturated fatty acid that is effective in reducing blood cholesterol levels. They are also low in calories and have been proven to increase the amount of friendly bacteria in the gut, so preventing constipation and reducing blood pressure. Soya bean products are high in isoflavones – a group of chemicals found in plant foods. They have a similar structure to the female hormone oestrogen and mimic the action of oestrogen that is naturally produced in the body. The isoflavones bind to oestrogen receptor sites in human cells including breast cells.

Soya also contains several types of antioxidants which help protect against and combat many serious diseases, including heart disease and some cancers. It is noteworthy that the increase in breast and prostate cancers is far lower in those countries with high soya consumption than in Britain and the United States, for example. Isoflavones, in combination with the high levels of calcium found in soya products, also help to maintain healthy bones and protect against osteoporosis. In addition, tofu's high calcium content can help to relieve some of the symptoms associated with the menopause, in particular reducing hot flushes.

Types of tofu

Above: Tofu is an excellent meat substitute, and is a principal source of protein for vegetarians and vegans.

There is a surprisingly large range of different kinds of tofu available, but you may have to go to a Chinese or Japanese food store to buy some of the less familiar ones that are discussed below. It's worth visiting an Asian supermarket in any case, even when buying the most common kinds of tofu, as a consistent high quality is virtually guaranteed from these outlets.

FIRM TOFU

Also known as cotton-strained tofu because of the way it is made, this is the traditional Chinese tofu that is harder to crumble. It is shaped into blocks, measuring about 7.5cm/3in square and 2.5cm/1in thick. It is available fresh or in vacuum packs, which need to be drained before use. For best results, firm tofu should be pressed before use to remove the excess water (see page 18).

Firm tofu has a slightly grainy texture and needs gentle handling, as it will break into smaller pieces especially when cooked. To avoid this, you can blanch the pieces in boiling water or briefly fry them in oil to harden them before stir-frying or braising. Always use a sharp knife when slicing firm tofu, as a blunt blade will squash it and cause the tofu block to crumble.

Firm tofu that is vacuum-packed will keep for several weeks in the refrigerator. Once opened, fresh firm tofu should be kept submerged in water in a lidded plastic box in the refrigerator. Change the water daily and use the tofu within a week. Freezing is not recommended as this alters the texture of the tofu.

You can also get medium and soft tofu in blocks, the only difference being the length of time they have been pressed.

SILKEN TOFU

This is the original Japanese type of tofu, and is also known as silken-strained tofu. It has a finer texture than firm tofu and is available fresh and in long-life vacuum packs (as with firm tofu, drain vacuum-packed silken tofu before using).

Silken tofu is smooth and soft and breaks down easily, so is best added at the last minute to soups or sprinkled over stir-fries or salads.

Right: Clockwise from top left: seared (yaki–dofu), marinated, firm and silken tofu.

Fresh silken tofu should be stored in the refrigerator and used within one week. The vacuum-packed type does not need to be stored in the refrigerator. However, it should not be frozen.

Below: Soy sauce and Chinese five-spice powder are typically used to marinate tofu.

MARINATED TOFU
Also known as pressed tofu, marinated tofu is made by compressing fresh tofu until almost all of the liquid has been squeezed out, leaving a solid block with a smooth texture. The tofu is then marinated in a mixture of soy sauce and Chinese five-spice powder, which colours the outside a rich dark brown while the inside remains white. It is available in vacuum packs from Asian stores and can also be bought from some health-food stores and supermarkets.

It will keep for several weeks in the refrigerator, in an airtight container. However, it should not be frozen.

SMOKED TOFU
Firm tofu is also available smoked, which adds a distinctive flavour. It can be used in stir-fries and salads, and is also good in pasta and rice dishes. Smoked tofu will keep for up to one month in the refrigerator, but should not be frozen.

Above: Frozen tofu needs to be soaked in hot water for about five minutes before cooking. Squeeze out the milky liquid and then cook as preferred.

Opposite: Clockwise from top left: frozen tofu, uncooked deep-fried tofu sheets, and cooked deep-fried tofu cubes and sheets.

FROZEN TOFU

Freeze-dried, frozen tofu is different in every way from firm or silken tofu. It has a spongy texture and a rich flavour, even after soaking in water, and does not disintegrate however long it is cooked. The process of freezing and thawing is what produces its characteristic texture.

Frozen tofu is available from Japanese stores and is often sold in packets of five pieces together with a powdered soup stock in which to cook it. It may simply be called frozen tofu (or dofu) or labelled koya-dofu or koguri-dofu. If you buy it in a pack with soup stock, it can be cooked to produce an almost instant meal. It should be reconstituted before cooking by soaking it in very hot water for a few minutes. It will have swelled up to 3–4 times its size.

Unopened packets of frozen tofu will keep for a long time, but check and do not exceed the 'use by' date.

DEEP-FRIED TOFU

Although relatively mild in flavour, deep-fried tofu has an interesting texture. It is fresh firm tofu that has been cut into cubes or triangles and deep-fried in vegetable oil until golden brown. There are both Japanese and Chinese versions of deep-fried tofu that differ very slightly, but may be used interchangeably. Deep-fried tofu is available from larger supermarkets and Asian stores. It is quite robust and does not disintegrate during cooking. To reduce the oiliness, rinse deep-fried tofu in boiling water and pat dry with kitchen paper before cooking.

When cooked, deep-fried tofu puffs up so that the golden, crisp coating becomes a somewhat baggy casing for the creamy white tofu inside. The outer coating readily absorbs flavours and makes it best suited to marinating in, dressing with or dipping into strong-flavoured sauces, especially those containing soy sauce and chilli. Deep-fried tofu sheets (known in Japanese cuisine as aburaage) can be cooked by boiling in water for a few minutes and then filled with a variety of ingredients such as fresh sushi, stir-fried vegetables or rice.

Deep-fried tofu does not keep well as it becomes soggy. However, it can be crisped again by baking, stir-frying, grilling or broiling and can be frozen for up to one year.

OTHER BEAN CURD PRODUCTS

Arguably, Japan produces the widest range of soya bean products, but China, Korea and other Asian countries are close behind.

Bean curd skins: These are made from soya 'milk'. A large pan of the milk is slowly brought to the boil, then the thin layer of skin that forms on the surface is skimmed off with a stick in a single action and hung up to dry – a simple-sounding technique that requires considerable skill in practice. When dry, the milk forms a flat sheet or skin.

Bean curd skins should be soaked in water for 1–2 hours before cooking. Always press out the excess water after soaking. Like fresh tofu, they have little flavour and aroma of their own but readily absorb the flavours of other stronger ingredients during cooking. The skins are used predominately in stir-fries, soups and casseroles and, occasionally, as wrappers for spring rolls.

Store bean curd skins in their original packets or in a sealed plastic bag in a cool dry place or refrigerator, where they will keep well for several days. If you wish to keep the skins longer than this then it is better to freeze them.

Bean curd sticks: These are made in the same way as bean curd skins but when the skin is still warm, it is rolled up around a chop stick and left to dry.

Bean curd sticks require much longer soaking than the skins, and they should be soaked overnight. They have no taste of their own but will absorb the flavour of other ingredients. Bean curd skins are best chopped and added to a variety of vegetarian dishes or cooked with meat in braised dishes and casseroles.

They should be stored in a sealed plastic bag in a cool and dry place.

Tempeh: Similar to tofu, but with a nuttier, more savoury flavour and firmer texture, tempeh is an Indonesian speciality. It is made by fermenting cooked soya beans with a culture. It is available chilled or frozen from health-food stores and Asian supermarkets.

Like firm tofu, tempeh benefits from marinating and can be used in many of the same ways – in stir-fries and kebabs, for example. However, its firmer texture also makes it an excellent meat rather than dairy substitute, so it is perfect in casseroles and baked dishes such as pies.

Chilled tempeh can be stored in the refrigerator for up to a week. Frozen tempeh can be stored in the freezer for a month and should be thawed completely before using.

Textured vegetable protein: This was specifically designed as a replacement for meat and is made from processed soya beans. Textured vegetable protein (TVP) is usually sold in dry chunks or minced (ground) and is widely available from Asian stores and large supermarkets.

TVP needs to be rehydrated with boiling water or stock before it is used in stews, curries or as a filling for pies. It readily absorbs the flavours of other ingredients such as herbs and spices.

Stored in a cool, dry place, TVP will keep for a few months.

SOYA DAIRY PRODUCTS
Soya 'milk', 'cream', 'yogurt' and 'cheese' are available from health-food stores and supermarkets and are ideal for vegans, people who prefer not to eat dairy products and anyone with a lactose intolerance.

Made from the pulverized beans, soya milk is the most widely used alternative to milk. It is slightly thicker than cow's milk and has a nutty flavour. Soya milk is lactose-free, low in fat and free of cholesterol, thereby offering positive health benefits. It is suitable for both cooking and drinking and is used to make yogurt, cream and cheese substitutes.

Soya cream is made with a higher proportion of beans than the milk, so it has a richer flavour and thicker texture. It has a similar consistency to single (light) cream and can be used in the same way.

Soya cheese is made from a blend of processed beans and vegetable fats and may be flavoured with herbs and spices. It can lack the depth of flavour of cheese made from cow's, goat's or sheep's milk, but may be used in the same ways. Store in the refrigerator.

Above: Clockwise from left: Soya yogurt, cream, milk and cheese.

Opposite top: Clockwise from left: Textured vegetable protein, bean curd skins and tempeh.

Opposite bottom: Bean curd sticks.

Cooking with tofu

Above: Tofu's soft texture means that it can be torn by hand, mashed with a fork, cut or sliced to suit the dish.

Tofu is an incredibly adaptable ingredient and works well in most cuisines. It is best known in Chinese and Japanese cooking where it is eaten plain or marinated, coated in flour and deep-fried or roasted, added to fragrant soups or stir-fried. The global vegetarian food culture has also seen an increasingly imaginative use of tofu, with chefs developing recipes ranging from burgers to creamy dressings and sweet desserts. It also features in the cooking of the Pacific Rim which innovatively marries flavours from East and West with thoroughly delectable results.

The subtle flavour and soft texture means that tofu can be added to all kinds of dishes without clashing with other ingredients. Tofu is also very sensitive to stronger flavours and is perfect for marinating, quickly becoming infused with a delicious depth of taste.

Firm tofu can be cubed or sliced for use in stir-fries, on skewers or in casseroles, curries, soups and salads. It can also be mashed and used in baked dishes and burgers.

Although silken tofu can also be used in soups and casseroles it really comes into its own when used to make sauces, dips, salad dressings and sweet fools or whips, as it imparts a rich creamy texture and takes on intense flavours.

In fact, it is the perfect low-fat alternative to cream, soft cheese, crème fraîche and yogurt and can be used as a substitute for traditional dairy products in many recipes. This is especially useful to those people who are lactose intolerant and for vegans.

Marinated tofu offers a contrast in both texture and flavour when combined with other ingredients. It can be used in a similar way to firm tofu, shredded or cut into thin slices and stir-fried with meat and/or vegetables. Marinated tofu is also a good choice for kebabs and can be added to casseroles, soups and stews.

Before cooking with frozen tofu it should be soaked in hot water for 5 minutes. Squeeze out the milky water a few times until it becomes clear. The tofu can then be simply eaten as it is or cooked with other ingredients. Typically it is simmered with vegetables and shiitake mushrooms in a rich soup or stew and is used for Buddhist monk's vegetarian cooking, known as shojin ryori.

Deep-fried tofu is used in the same way as firm tofu in soups, casseroles, stir-fries and braised dishes, and features in some Japanese seaweed recipes. Japanese thin deep-fried tofu sheets can be slit open in the same way as pitta bread and stuffed with minced pork, chicken, fish or prawns, then braised in a sauce. Japanese thick deep-fried tofu is fried as a whole block, so is only brown on the outside, while the inside remains delicately white.

Preparing tofu

While cooking with tofu, tempeh and other soya products is not difficult, there are useful techniques for handling these products that help to guarantee successful results. Tofu is very fragile and although the firm variety is more robust than silken tofu both should be handled with care to prevent crumbling during the cooking process.

PRESSING FIRM TOFU
Silken tofu is usually used as it is, but firm tofu needs to be pressed before cooking to squeeze out any excess water. This process makes the block firmer on the outside, and therefore ideal for deep-frying and stir-fries.

Unpack the tofu block and discard the liquid, then wrap the tofu in three layers of kitchen paper. Place a large plate on top of the tofu, put a weight, such as a heavy book, on it and leave the tofu to press for up to 1 hour, until all the excess water has been absorbed by the paper and the tofu is about half its original weight. Unwrap and pat dry with more pieces of kitchen paper.

SEARING FIRM TOFU
Briefly searing the outside of firm tofu helps to prevent it from disintegrating during stir-frying. Press the block of tofu first of all, as above.

Heat a griddle pan or heavy frying pan and brush with a little oil. When it is very hot, add the tofu and cook for a few seconds on each side, pressing it down gently in the pan. Remove the tofu from the pan and serve, either whole or cut into cubes, while still warm.

CUTTING FIRM TOFU
Firm tofu can be cut into slices or cubes. Always use a sharp knife when handling tofu as a blunt knife will squash the tofu and cause it to crumble.

Once the excess water has been drained from the block of firm tofu, pat it dry with kitchen paper. Place the tofu on a clean chopping board and cut the block into slices about 2cm/¾in thick or the required size for the recipe. If the recipe calls for cubes, cut the slices in half, and, finally, into even-sized cubes.

PAN-FRYING FIRM TOFU
Firm tofu is given a crisp texture on the outside but remains soft on the inside if it is pan-fried.

First press the block of tofu and slice into even-sized cubes. Preheat 30ml/1 tbsp groundnut or peanut oil in a wok or large frying pan and fry the tofu for 4–5 minutes until golden brown, turning occasionally. Use a slotted spoon to remove the cubes and drain on kitchen paper. Set the fried cubes aside until needed.

DEEP-FRYING FIRM TOFU
For a lovely crisp texture, cubes of firm tofu can also be deep-fried before combining with other ingredients in a dish.

First press the block of tofu and slice into even-sized cubes. Half-fill a wok with oil and heat to 180–190°C/ 350–375°F or until a cube of day-old bread browns in 30 seconds. Add the tofu cubes and deep-fry, turning once, for a few minutes, until light golden brown. Remove the pieces with a slotted spoon and drain on kitchen paper. Do not overcrowd the wok.

PREPARING THIN DEEP-FRIED TOFU
Thin sheets of deep-fried tofu, called aburaage, are used primarily in Japanese cooking.

Place the deep-fried tofu in a sieve and pour boiling water over them to wash off any excess oil. Drain off the water and pat dry with kitchen paper. Par-boil in rapidly boiling water for 1 minute, then drain and leave to cool. Squeeze out any excess water.

Place the tofu sheets on a chopping board and cut each sheet in half.

Carefully pull each half sheet open by rubbing the outside back and forth with the palm of your hand to ease the sides apart. Use your fingers to open the bag fully, working your way carefully towards the bottom. If the bags are not opening easily, gently insert a round-bladed knife into the bag and work around the bag opening it out gradually. Take care not to tear the sides.

Once the bags have been filled gently press the edges together to close the bag.

PROCESSING SILKEN TOFU
Silken tofu does not need to be pressed and can be used straight out of the packaging. Place the silken tofu into the bowl of a food processor or blender. Use a wooden spoon or the back of a fork to break the tofu into smaller pieces, then process or blend the tofu until it is at the required consistency for the recipe.

DRAINING TEMPEH
Although it has a firmer texture than tofu, tempeh also benefits from draining before cooking. Place the tempeh in a wire sieve set over a bowl and leave it to drain until the excess liquid has collected in the bowl. If using frozen tempeh, you can thaw and drain it simultaneously in the refrigerator or in a cool place.

MARINATING TEMPEH
Although tempeh has a nuttier, more savoury flavour, it still benefits from marinating. Use a mixture of flavoured oils, aromatic ingredients and spices and marinate for 1 hour.

CUTTING TEMPEH
If you use a sharp knife, you should have no problems cutting tempeh into cubes. Cut the tempeh into slices that are 1–2cm/½–¾in thick, then cut the slices in half and, finally, into cubes.

Tofu marinades

Tofu in its raw state is relatively tasteless and is at its best when marinated in strongly flavoured seasonings. Firm tofu is perfect for marinating, as it has a porous nature that absorbs flavours quickly and easily.

It is best to blanch the tofu first. Bring a large pan of water to the boil, and add a pinch of salt. Place the block of tofu in the water, being careful not to let it break apart. Blanch the tofu for 3 minutes. Remove and place on kitchen paper to remove any excess water. Transfer the tofu to a plate, and cover with the required dressing and marinate for at least 1 hour. Serve, slicing or cubing the tofu as desired.

The quantities below are sufficient for approximately 225g/8oz firm tofu.

Spicy soy marinade: 10ml/2 tsp finely sliced spring onion (scallion), 5ml/1 tsp finely chopped garlic, 60ml/4 tbsp dark soy sauce, 10ml/2 tsp chilli powder, 5ml/1 tsp sugar, and 10ml/2 tsp sesame seeds.

Chinese red marinade: 45ml/3 tbsp dark soy sauce, 30ml/2 tbsp Chinese rice wine, 15ml/1 tbsp grated fresh root ginger, 1 crushed garlic clove, 10ml/2 tsp soft dark brown sugar, 2.5ml/½ tsp Chinese five-spice powder and a pinch of ground, roasted Sichuan peppercorns.

Fresh herb marinade: 30ml/2 tbsp olive oil, 50ml/2fl oz dry white wine, 7.5ml/1½ tsp lemon juice and 15ml/1 tbsp chopped fresh herbs such as parsley, coriander (cilantro), basil and thyme. Season with black pepper.

Spicy Indian marinade: ½ finely chopped medium-sized onion, 1 crushed garlic clove, 2.5ml/½ tsp grated fresh root ginger, 2.5ml/½ tsp ground cumin, 2.5ml/½ tsp ground coriander, 1.5ml/¼ tsp ground turmeric and 75ml/5 tbsp natural (plain) yogurt.

Mustard marinade: 15ml/1 tbsp ready-made English (hot) mustard, 30ml/2 tbsp sugar, 15ml/1 tbsp milk, 45ml/3 tbsp cider vinegar, 5ml/1 tsp chilli oil, 2.5ml/½ tsp dark soy sauce, 5ml/1 tsp salt.

SOUPS, SNACKS & STARTERS

Light, delicate and versatile, tofu is the perfect choice for the first course as it stimulates the appetite. Tofu is also a handy ingredient for a wide range of tasty snacks from deep-fried crab cakes and tofu spring rolls to spicy soups and delicious dips.

SERVES 4

1.2 litres/2 pints/4 cups vegetable stock

5–10ml/1–2 tsp Thai red curry paste

2 kaffir lime leaves, torn

40g/1½ oz/3 tbsp palm sugar or light muscovado (brown) sugar

30ml/2 tbsp light soy sauce

juice of 1 lime

1 carrot, cut into thin batons

50g/2oz baby spinach leaves, any coarse stalks removed

225g/8oz silken tofu, rinsed and diced

Hot-and-sweet vegetable and tofu soup

An interesting combination of hot sweet and sour flavours that makes for a soothing nutritious soup. It is quick to make as the spinach and tofu are simply placed in bowls and covered with the well-flavoured hot stock.

1 Heat the stock in a large pan, then add the red curry paste. Stir constantly over a medium heat until the paste has dissolved. Add the lime leaves, sugar and soy sauce and bring to the boil.

2 Add the lime juice and carrot to the pan. Reduce the heat and simmer for 5–10 minutes. Place the spinach and tofu in four individual serving bowls and pour the hot stock on top to serve.

Vegetable and marinated fried tofu soup

This satisfying and appealing soup is a meal in itself and can be adapted to use whatever vegetables are available. It is especially tasty if made with fresh seasonal produce, the marinated deep-fried tofu adding extra richness.

1 Preheat the oven to 200°C/400°F/Gas 6. Heat the oil in a large pan then sauté the leeks, celery and garlic for 7–8 minutes, or until softened and beginning to turn golden .

2 Add the other vegetables and dried herbs. Stir to mix well, then pour over the vegetable stock and canned tomatoes. Bring to the boil, then simmer for 20–25 minutes.

3 Meanwhile, place the tofu pieces on a baking sheet and bake for 8–10 minutes to warm through.

4 Add the chopped parsley or basil to the soup and season to taste with sea salt and pepper. Stir in the warmed tofu and serve.

SERVES 4

15ml/1 tbsp olive oil
2 leeks, finely chopped
2 celery sticks, finely diced
2 garlic cloves, finely chopped
2 courgette (zucchini), finely diced
450g/1lb carrots, finely diced
200g/7oz green beans, finely sliced
5ml/1 tsp dried Mediterranean herbs
1.2 litres/2 pints/5 cups vegetable stock
400g/14oz can chopped tomatoes
300g/11oz marinated deep-fried tofu pieces
20g/¾oz bunch fat leaf parsley or basil, chopped
sea salt and ground black pepper

Miso broth with spring onions and tofu

The Japanese eat miso broth, a simple but highly nutritious soup, almost every day – it is standard breakfast fare and it is also eaten with rice or noodles later in the day. Here it is made into a more fulsome meal with the addition of tofu.

1 Cut the coarse green tops off the spring onions or baby leeks and set aside. Slice the rest of the spring onions or leeks finely on the diagonal and set aside. Place the coarse green tops in a large pan with the coriander stalks, fresh root ginger, star anise, dried chilli and dashi or vegetable stock.

2 Heat the mixture gently until boiling, then lower the heat and simmer for about 10 minutes. Strain, return to the pan and reheat until simmering. Add the green portion of the sliced spring onions or leeks to the soup with the pak choi or greens and tofu. Cook for 2 minutes.

3 Mix 45ml/3 tbsp of the miso with a little of the hot soup in a bowl, then stir it into the soup. Taste the soup and add more miso with soy sauce as needed to taste.

4 Coarsely chop the coriander leaves and stir most of them into the soup with the white part of the spring onions or leeks. Cook for 1 minute, then ladle the soup into warmed serving bowls. Sprinkle with the remaining coriander and the fresh red chilli, if using, and serve at once.

COOK'S TIP Dashi powder is available in most Asian and Chinese stores. Alternatively, make your own by gently simmering 10–15cm/ 4–6in kombu seaweed in 1.2 litres/2 pints/5 cups water for 10 minutes. Do not boil the stock vigorously as this makes the dashi bitter. Remove the kombu, then add 15g/½ oz dried bonito flakes and bring to the boil. Strain immediately through a fine sieve.

SERVES 4

1 bunch of spring onions (scallions) or 5 baby leeks
15g/½ oz fresh coriander (cilantro)
3 thin slices fresh root ginger
2 star anise
1 small dried red chilli
1.2 litres/2 pints/5 cups dashi stock or vegetable stock
225g/8oz pak choi (bok choy) or other Asian greens, thickly sliced
200g/7oz firm tofu, drained and cut into bitesize cubes
60ml/4 tbsp red miso
30–45ml/2–3 tbsp dark soy sauce
1 fresh red chilli, seeded and shredded (optional)

Tofu and bean sprout soup with rice noodles

SERVES 4

150g/5oz dried thick rice noodles

1 litre/1¾ pints/4 cups vegetable stock

1 red chilli, seeded and sliced

15ml/1 tbsp light soy sauce

juice of 1 small lime

10ml/2 tsp palm sugar

5ml/1 tsp finely sliced garlic

5ml/1 tsp finely chopped fresh root ginger

200g/7oz firm tofu, drained and cut into bitesize cubes

90g/3½oz mung bean sprouts

30ml/2 tbsp chopped fresh mint

15ml/1 tbsp chopped fresh coriander (cilantro)

15ml/1 tbsp chopped fresh sweet basil

50g/2oz roasted peanuts, roughly chopped

spring onion (scallion) slivers and red (bell) pepper slivers, to garnish

This light and refreshing soup is very quick and simple to make. The aromatic, spicy broth is simmered first, before adding the tofu, bean sprouts and noodles for very brief cooking. Make sure you use firm tofu because the softer variety will disintegrate during cooking.

1 Place the noodles in a bowl and pour over enough boiling water to cover. Soak for 10–15 minutes, until soft. Drain, rinse and set aside.

2 Meanwhile, place the stock, red chilli, soy sauce, lime juice, sugar, garlic and ginger in a wok over a high heat. Bring to the boil, cover, reduce to a low heat and simmer gently for 10–12 minutes.

3 Add the drained noodles, tofu and mung bean sprouts and cook gently for 2–3 minutes. Remove from the heat and stir in the chopped herbs.

4 Ladle the soup into bowls and scatter over the peanuts. Garnish with spring onion and red pepper slivers.

SERVES 4

300g/11oz firm tofu, drained
and cut into bitesize cubes
30ml/2 tbsp groundnut
(peanut) oil
1.2 litres/2 pints/5 cups good
vegetable stock
15ml/1 tbsp Thai chilli jam
grated rind of 1 kaffir lime
1 shallot, thinly sliced
1 garlic clove, finely chopped
2 kaffir lime leaves, shredded
3 red chillies, seeded and
shredded
1 lemon grass stalk, finely
chopped
6 shiitaki mushrooms, thinly
sliced
4 spring onions (scallions),
shredded
45ml/3 tbsp Thai fish sauce
45ml/3 tbsp lime juice
5ml/1 tsp caster (superfine)
sugar
45ml/3 tbsp chopped fresh
coriander (cilantro)
salt and ground black pepper

Tom yam gung with tofu

One of the most refreshing and healthy soups, this fragrant
and colourful dish is a Thai speciality.

1 Heat the oil in a wok, add the tofu and cook over a medium
heat, turning occasionally, for about 4–5 minutes, until golden.
Use a slotted spoon to remove it and set aside. Tip the oil from
the wok into a large heavy pan.

2 Add the stock, chilli jam, kaffir lime rind, shallot, garlic, lime
leaves, two-thirds of the chillies and the lemon grass to the pan.
Bring to the boil, lower the heat and simmer for 20 minutes.

3 Strain the stock into a clean pan. Stir in the remaining chilli, the
shiitaki mushrooms, spring onions, Thai fish sauce, lime juice and
sugar. Simmer for 3 minutes. Add the fried tofu and heat through
for 1 minute. Mix in the chopped coriander and season to taste.
Serve immediately in warmed bowls.

COOK'S TIP Fresh kaffir limes and leaves are available from South-east
Asian stores. If you cannot find them, use freeze-dried leaves, which are
widely available, or grated ordinary lime rind.

Potato wedges with tofu dip

Tofu makes a fabulous dip that is cool and creamy – the perfect foil for crispy hot potato wedges.

1 Cut the potatoes lengthways in half, then cut each half lengthways into thirds or quarters to make wedges. Place them in a shallow dish and sprinkle over the spices, citrus rind, oil and seasoning. Toss together and leave to marinate for at least 30 minutes. Meanwhile, preheat the oven to 220°C/425°F/Gas 7.

2 Place the potato wedges in a roasting pan and bake for 30–35 minutes, until golden and tender, turning occasionally.

3 Meanwhile, make the garlic tofu dip by placing all the ingredients, except the oil, in a blender or food processor and processing until smooth.

4 With the machine running, gradually add the olive oil in a slow, steady stream until the dip is smooth and thickened. Season with salt and pepper to taste, then pour into a serving bowl. Transfer the potato wedges to a warm serving dish and serve with the dip.

COOK'S TIP If covered, the dip will keep in the refrigerator for up to 1 week.

SERVES 4

6 potatoes, scrubbed
15ml/1 tbsp cumin seeds, ground
2.5–5ml/½–1 tsp cayenne pepper
grated rind of 2 limes or 1 lemon
45ml/3 tbsp olive oil
sea salt and ground black pepper

For the garlic tofu dip
1 garlic clove, crushed
175g/6oz silken tofu
dash of lemon juice
10g/¼oz fresh mint, stalks removed (optional)
25ml/1½ tbsp olive oil

Spicy soft tofu and seafood stew

The underlying fiery spiciness of this dish really helps to emphasize its seafood flavours. Clams and prawns are served in a piquant soup with a medley of vegetables, with creamy tofu melting into the rich sauce.

1 Break the block of tofu into small pieces with your hands, place them in a bowl and marinate with the soy sauce and a pinch of salt for about 1 hour.

2 Scrub the clams in cold running water. Discard the caps from the enoki mushrooms.

3 In a flameproof casserole dish or heavy pan, heat the vegetable oil over a high heat. Add the chopped beef and stir-fry until the meat has browned.

4 Add the chilli powder, garlic and a splash of water to the pan. Stir-fry, coating the meat with the spices. Add the water or stock and bring to the boil.

5 Add the clams, prawns and tofu, and boil for a further 4 minutes.

6 Reduce the heat slightly and add the leek, chillies and mushrooms. Continue to cook until the leek has softened. Then stir in the dark soy sauce and Thai fish sauce. Season with salt if necessary, and serve.

SERVES 2–3

300g/11oz soft tofu, drained
15ml/1 tbsp light soy sauce
6 clams
25g/1oz enoki mushrooms
15ml/1 tbsp vegetable oil
50g/2oz beef, finely chopped
7.5ml/1½ tsp Korean chilli powder
5ml/1 tsp crushed garlic
500ml/17fl oz/generous 2 cups water or beef stock
6 peeled raw prawns (shrimp)
⅓ leek, sliced
½ red chilli, sliced
½ green chilli, sliced
2.5ml/½ tsp dark soy sauce
1.5ml/¼ tsp Thai fish sauce
salt

Tofu spring rolls

MAKES 12

6 Chinese dried mushrooms, soaked for 30 minutes in warm water
150g/5oz firm tofu, drained
30ml/2 tbsp sunflower oil
225g/8oz finely minced (ground) pork
225g/8oz peeled cooked prawns (shrimp), coarsely chopped
2.5ml/½ tsp cornflour (cornstarch), mixed to a paste with 15ml/1 tbsp light soy sauce
75g/3oz shredded bamboo shoots or grated carrot
75g/3oz sliced water chestnuts
75g/3oz beansprouts
6 spring onions (scallions) or 1 young leek, finely chopped
a little sesame oil
12 spring roll wrappers, thawed if frozen
30ml/2 tbsp plain (all-purpose) flour, mixed to a paste with water
sunflower oil, for deep-frying

For the dipping sauce
100ml/3½fl oz/scant ½ cup light soy sauce
15ml/1 tbsp chilli sauce
a little sesame oil
rice vinegar, to taste

Spring rolls are delicious at any time of day and these tofu, mushroom and prawn-filled versions are going to be hard to beat. Not only will they be delicious, the firm tofu adds extra protein to the mixture. A classic Chinese snack, it is said that spring rolls were traditionally served with tea when visitors came to call after the Chinese New Year. As this was springtime, they came to be known as spring rolls. Buy fresh or frozen spring roll wrappers from Asian stores.

1 To make the filling, drain the mushrooms. Cut off and discard the stems and slice the caps finely. Slice the tofu thinly.

2 Heat the oil in a wok and stir-fry the pork for 2–3 minutes, or until the colour changes. Add the prawns, cornflour paste and bamboo shoot or carrot. Stir in the water chestnuts.

3 Increase the heat, add the beansprouts and spring onions or leek and toss for 1 minute. Stir in the mushrooms and tofu. Remove the wok from the heat, season, then stir in the sesame oil. Cool quickly on a large platter.

4 Separate the spring roll wrappers. Place a wrapper on the work surface with one corner nearest you. Spoon some of the filling near the centre of the wrapper and fold the nearest corner over the filling. Brush a little of the flour paste on the free sides, turn the sides into the middle and roll up the wrapper to enclose the filling. Repeat with the remaining wrappers and filling.

5 Deep-fry the spring rolls, in batches, in oil heated to 190°C/375°F until they are crisp and golden. Drain on kitchen paper and serve immediately with the dipping sauce, made by mixing all the ingredients in a bowl.

Deep-fried fish and tofu cakes

Well-made fishcakes are always a treat, and they can be made with any fresh or smoked white fish. The addition of smooth soft tofu ensures the mixture is extra creamy and makes a little fish go a long way.

1 Steam the fish for 10 minutes, then cool, flake and mash until fine. Thoroughly mix the tofu and egg with the fish, cornflour and rice flour.

2 Add the spring onions, garlic, sesame oil, soy sauce and pepper. Stir well and shape into small patties about 4cm/1½in in diameter and 1cm/½in thick. Deep-fry until golden brown, and serve with sliced cucumber and chilli sauce.

VARIATION For a vegetarian alternative, use a mixture of minced or ground vegetables, such as mushrooms, marrow, large zucchini and carrots alongside the soft tofu.

SERVES 4

350g/12oz meaty white fish, such as cod or halibut
115g/4oz soft tofu, drained and mashed
1 egg, lightly beaten
15ml/1 tbsp cornflour (cornstarch)
15ml/1 tbsp rice flour
2 spring onions (scallions), finely chopped
3 garlic cloves, crushed
15ml/1 tbsp sesame oil
15ml/1 tbsp light soy sauce
2.5ml/½ tsp ground black pepper
vegetable oil, for deep-frying
thinly sliced cucumber and chilli sauce, to serve

Sushi rice in tofu bags

SERVES 1

8 slices of deep-fried tofu
sheets
900ml/1½ pints/3¾ cups water
and 10ml/2 tsp dashi-no-moto
(Japanese stock granules)
90ml/6 tbsp caster (superfine)
sugar
30ml/2 tbsp sake (Japanese
rice wine)
70ml/4½ tbsp dark soy sauce
generous 1 quantity sushi rice,
made with 40ml/8 tsp sugar
30ml/2 tbsp toasted white
sesame seeds
gari, to garnish (see Cook's
Tip)

These delightful little tofu pockets are served with soy sauce-
based seasonings and filled with sushi rice.

1 Par-boil the deep-fried tofu sheets in rapidly boiling water for
about 1 minute. Drain under cold running water and leave to
cool. Squeeze the excess water out gently. Cut each sheet in half
and carefully pull open the cut end to make bags.

2 Lay the tofu bags in a large pan. Pour in the dashi stock to
cover and bring to the boil. Reduce the heat and cover, then
simmer for 20 minutes. Add the sugar in three batches during
this time, shaking the pan to dissolve it. Simmer for a further
15 minutes.

3 Add the sake. Shake the pan again, and add the soy sauce in
three batches. Simmer until almost all the liquid has evaporated.
Transfer the tofu bags to a wide sieve and leave to drain.

4 Mix the sushi rice and sesame seeds in a wet mixing bowl. Wet
your hands, take a little of the mixture and shape it into a
rectangular block. Open one tofu bag and insert the block. Press
the edges together to close the bag.

5 Once all the bags have been filled, place them on a large
serving plate or individual plates with the bottom of the bag on
top. Garnish with a little gari.

COOK'S TIP Gari are pale pink ginger pickles available from Japanese
food stores. They have a pleasantly refreshing flavour.

Deep-fried tofu balls

There are many variations of these delicious Japanese deep-fried tofu balls called hiryozu, meaning flying dragon's head. This is one of the easiest to make.

1 To make the tofu balls, chop the carrot finely. Trim and cut the beans into 5mm/¼in lengths. Cook both vegetables for 1 minute in boiling water.

2 In a food processor, process the tofu, eggs, sake, mirin, salt, soy sauce and sugar until smooth. Transfer to a bowl and mix in the carrot and beans.

3 Fill a wok or pan with oil 4cm/1½in deep, and heat to 185°C/365°F.

4 Soak a piece of kitchen paper with a little vegetable oil, and rub your hands with it. Scoop 40ml/2½ tbsp of the tofu mixture in one hand and shape into a ball by tossing it between your hands.

5 Deep-fry the tofu ball until crisp and golden brown. Drain on kitchen paper. Repeat shaping and deep-frying with the remaining mixture.

6 Arrange the tofu balls on a serving plate and sprinkle with chives. Mix the lime sauce ingredients in a serving bowl. Serve the balls with the lime sauce.

20g/¾oz carrot, peeled
40g/1½oz green beans
600g/1lb 6oz firm tofu, drained and hand torn into large pieces
2 large (US extra large) eggs, beaten
30ml/2 tbsp sake (Japanese rice wine)
10ml/2 tsp mirin (sweet rice wine)
5ml/1 tsp salt
10ml/2 tsp dark soy sauce
pinch of caster (superfine) sugar
vegetable oil, for deep-frying
4 chives, finely chopped, to garnish

For the lime sauce
45ml/3 tbsp soy sauce
juice of ½ lime
5ml/1 tsp rice vinegar

Tofu falafel with hummus

SERVES 4–6

30ml/2 tbsp vegetable oil
2 large onions, finely chopped
3 garlic cloves, crushed
500g/1¼lb firm tofu, drained and cut into bitesize cubes
200g/7oz/3¾ cups fresh breadcrumbs
15g/½oz bunch fresh parsley, finely chopped
15ml/1 tbsp roasted sesame oil
45ml/3 tbsp light soy sauce
50g/2oz/4 tbsp sesame seeds, toasted
5ml/1 tsp ground cumin
15ml/1 tbsp ground turmeric
60ml/4 tbsp tahini
juice of 1 lemon
1.5ml/¼ tsp cayenne pepper

For the hummus
150g/5oz/¾ cup dried chickpeas
juice of 2 lemons
2 garlic cloves, sliced
30ml/2 tbsp olive oil
pinch of cayenne pepper
150ml/¼ pint/⅔ cup tahini
salt and ground black pepper
extra olive oil and cayenne pepper, for sprinkling
flat leaf parsley, to garnish

Fresh, lightly spiced home-made hummus goes perfectly with these delicious, crunchy tofu balls. Serve with warm pitta bread and a sweet chilli dip, if you like.

1 To make the hummus, put the chickpeas in a bowl, pour in plenty of cold water to cover, then leave to soak overnight.

2 Drain the chickpeas and place in a pan. Add fresh cold water to cover, bring to the boil and boil rapidly for 10 minutes. Reduce the heat and simmer gently for about 1–1½ hours, until tender. You may need to cook the chickpeas for longer, depending on how long they have been stored. Drain.

3 Meanwhile make the tofu falafel. Heat the vegetable oil in a large frying pan and sauté the onion and garlic over a medium heat for 2–3 minutes, until softened. Set aside to cool slightly.

4 Preheat the oven to 180°C/350°F/Gas 4. In a large bowl, mix together the remaining ingredients until well blended, then stir in the onion mixture.

5 Form the mixture into 2.5cm/1in diameter balls and place them on an oiled baking sheet. Bake for 30 minutes, or until crusty on the outside but still moist on the inside.

6 Meanwhile, place the chickpeas in a food processor and process to a smooth purée, pulsing the machine and scraping down the chickpeas once or twice. Add the lemon juice, garlic, olive oil, cayenne pepper and tahini and blend until smooth and creamy, scraping the mixture down from the sides of the bowl.

7 Season the purée with salt and pepper to taste and transfer the hummus to a serving dish. Sprinkle with olive oil and cayenne pepper and garnish with a few parsley sprigs. Serve with the hot falafel, speared with cocktail sticks (toothpicks).

COOK'S TIP For convenience, canned chickpeas can be used instead. Allow two 400g/14oz cans and drain them thoroughly. Rinse well under cold running water and drain again before processing.

Tofu and seafood wontons

Wontons are a popular Chinese street snack, containing many different fillings. Here a heady combination of shellfish and creamy soft tofu combine to make a satisfying snack. Wontons are very easy to make and lend themselves to deep-frying, steaming or adding to soups. It is important to work quickly when using wonton skins – after making the wontons, do not let them stand for too long before cooking, as the skins can become brittle when exposed to the air.

1 Wash the prawns and then mince or grind them very finely. Mix with the crab meat and mashed tofu, then add the beaten egg and mix until well combined.

2 Add the soy sauce, sesame oil, black pepper and cornflour. Stir again and divide into 16 equal portions.

3 Put one portion of the mixture on to a wonton skin and fold up into a half-moon shape, sealing the edge with a little water. (If the skins are square, fold them into triangles.) Repeat with the other wonton skins.

4 Either deep-fry the wontons until golden brown, or steam them for 10 minutes. Serve with a chilli sauce dip.

COOK'S TIP Wonton skins are made from flour and are available in all Chinese stores, either as 7.5cm/3in squares or circles of the same diameter.

SERVES 4

250g/9oz peeled raw prawns (shrimp)
250g/9oz white crab meat
115g/4oz soft tofu, drained and finely mashed
1 egg, lightly beaten
30ml/2 tbsp light soy sauce
15ml/1 tbsp sesame oil
2.5ml/½ tsp ground black pepper
5ml/1 tsp cornflour (cornstarch)
16 wonton skins
vegetable oil, for deep-frying (optional)
chilli sauce, to serve

Thai tempeh cakes with dipping sauce

MAKES 8

1 lemon grass stalk, outer leaves removed and inside chopped

2 garlic cloves, chopped

2 spring onions (scallions), chopped

2 shallots, chopped

2 chillies, seeded and chopped

2:5cm/1in piece fresh root ginger, chopped

60ml/4 tbsp chopped fresh coriander (cilantro), plus extra to garnish

250g/9oz tempeh, thawed if frozen, sliced

15ml/1 tbsp lime juice

5ml/1 tsp sugar

45ml/3 tbsp plain (all-purpose) flour

1 large (US extra large) egg, lightly beaten

vegetable oil, for frying

salt and ground black pepper

For the dipping sauce

45ml/3 tbsp mirin (see Cook's Tip)

45ml/3 tbsp white wine vinegar

2 spring onions (scallions), thinly sliced

15ml/1 tbsp sugar

2 chillies, finely chopped

30ml/2 tbsp chopped fresh coriander (cilantro), plus extra to garnish

large pinch of salt

Here, nutty-tasting tempeh is combined with a fragrant blend of lemon grass, fresh coriander and ginger and formed into small patties before being fried.

1 To make the dipping sauce, mix together the mirin, vinegar, spring onions, sugar, chillies, coriander and salt in a small bowl and set aside.

2 Place the lemon grass, garlic, spring onions, shallots, chillies, ginger and coriander in a food processor or blender and process to a coarse paste. Add the tempeh, lime juice and sugar, then process to combine. Add the seasoning, flour and egg. Process again until the mixture forms a coarse, sticky paste.

3 Take one-eighth of the tempeh mixture at a time and form into balls with your hands – the mixture will be quite sticky, so it may help to dampen your palms. Gently flatten the balls.

4 Heat enough oil to cover the base of a large frying pan. Fry the tempeh cakes for 5–6 minutes, turning once, until golden. Drain on kitchen paper. Garnish with chopped coriander and serve warm with the dipping sauce.

COOK'S TIP Mirin is a sweet sake, or rice wine, with a delicate flavour. It is designed to be used for cooking and is relatively inexpensive. It is available from Japanese food stores and some large supermarkets.

Pan-fried tofu with caramelized sauce

Tofu is the perfect ingredient for marinating in a tasty sauce as it absorbs flavours so well. This satisfying dish is a modern take on the vegetarian cuisine developed by Buddhist monks in Japan. If you don't have mirin, you can use Amontillado sherry instead.

1 Slice the tofu into 1.5cm/1in cubes.

2 To make the marinade, chop the spring onions finely. Mix with the other marinade ingredients in a ceramic or aluminium tray with sides or a wide, shallow bowl. Soak the tofu cubes in the marinade for 15 minutes.

3 Slice the garlic very thinly to make garlic chips. Heat the vegetable oil in a frying pan or wok and cook the garlic for a few moments until golden. Turn the garlic chips frequently to prevent them from sticking and burning. Scoop them out on to kitchen paper to drain. Reserve the oil in the pan.

4 Take out the tofu and wipe off the excess marinade with kitchen paper. Reserve the marinade.

5 Reheat the oil in the frying pan and add one piece of butter. When the oil starts sizzling, reduce the heat to medium and add the pieces of tofu one by one. Cook in one layer, if possible.

6 Cover the pan and cook for about 5–8 minutes on each side, until the edge of the tofu is browned and quite firm. (If the edges burn but the centre is pale, reduce the heat.)

7 Pour the marinade into the pan. Cook for 2 minutes, or until the spring onion is very soft. Remove the tofu with a slotted spoon and arrange four pieces on each of four serving plates. Pour the thickened marinade and spring onion mixture over the tofu and top with a piece of butter. Sprinkle with the garlic chips and garnish with watercress sprigs. Serve while still hot.

SERVES 4

600g/1lb 6oz firm tofu, drained
4 garlic cloves
10ml/2 tsp vegetable oil
50g/2oz/¼ cup butter, cut into 5 equal pieces
watercress, to garnish

For the marinade
4 spring onions (scallions)
60ml/4 tbsp sake (Japanese rice wine)
60ml/4 tbsp dark soy sauce
60ml/4 tbsp mirin (sweet rice wine)

Stuffed pan-fried tofu

SERVES 2

600g/1lb 6oz firm tofu, drained
30ml/2 tbsp Thai fish sauce
5ml/1 tsp sesame oil
2 eggs
7.5ml/1½ tsp cornflour
(cornstarch)
vegetable oil, for shallow-
frying

For the filling
2 green chillies, finely chopped
2 chestnuts, finely chopped
6 garlic cloves, crushed
10ml/2 tsp sesame seeds

An easy accompaniment for a main course, or a great appetizer. Squares of fried tofu stuffed with a blend of chilli and chestnut give a piquant jolt to the delicate flavour. The tofu has a crispy coating, surrounding a creamy texture, with a crunchy filling.

1 Cut the tofu into 2cm/¾in slices and then cut each slice in half. Place the tofu slices on pieces of kitchen paper to blot and absorb any excess water.

2 Mix together the Thai fish sauce and sesame oil. Transfer the tofu slices to a plate and coat them with the fish sauce mixture. Leave to marinate for 20 minutes. Meanwhile, put all the filling ingredients into a bowl and combine them thoroughly. Set aside.

3 Beat the eggs in a shallow dish. Add the cornflour and whisk until well combined. Take the slices of tofu and dip them into the beaten egg mixture, ensuring an even coating on all sides.

4 Place a frying pan or wok over a medium heat and add some vegetable oil. Add the tofu slices to the pan and sauté, turning over once, until they are golden brown.

5 Once cooked, make a slit down the middle of each slice with a sharp knife, without cutting all the way through. Gently stuff a large pinch of the filling into each slice, and serve.

VARIATION Alternatively, you can serve the tofu with a light soy dip instead of the spicy filling.

SALADS & SIDES

Silken tofu is an invaluable ingredient for making creamy dressings and sauces, whether in a rich-tasting egg-free mayonnaise combined with spiralized vegetables or a herb-infused tofu pesto. Firm tofu provides a great contrast of texture and appearance in salad leaves and cooked vegetables.

Tofu, broccoli and mushroom salad

SERVES 4

250g/9oz firm, or smoked tofu, drained and cut into bitesize cubes
250g/9oz broccoli, cut into large florets
15ml/1 tbsp olive oil
1 garlic clove, finely chopped
350g/12oz chestnut mushrooms, sliced
4 spring onions (scallions), thinly sliced
75g/3oz/¾ cup pine nuts, toasted

For the marinade
1 garlic clove, crushed
2.5cm/1in piece fresh root ginger, finely grated
45ml/3 tbsp light soy sauce
45ml/3 tbsp tamari soy sauce
45ml/3 tbsp Chinese rice wine or dry sherry
1.5ml/¼ tsp cumin seeds, toasted and coarsely crushed
1.5ml/¼ tsp caster (superfine) sugar
ground black pepper

This bold-flavoured salad combines satisfyingly contrasting textures in the tofu and vegetables. It could be served with buckwheat and a pinch of dried chilli flakes to make a delicious meal.

1 Prepare the marinade by stirring all the ingredients together in a jug or pitcher. Place the tofu cubes in a bowl, pour in the marinade, toss to coat and leave to marinate for at least 1 hour.

2 Meanwhile steam the broccoli for 4–5 minutes, until just tender then refresh under cold running water. Drain well then place in a large bowl.

3 Heat the oil in a large, heavy frying pan or wok. Add the garlic and stir-fry over a low heat for 1 minute, until golden. Do not allow the garlic to burn.

4 Add the mushrooms and fry over a high heat for 4–5 minutes, until cooked through. Add to the broccoli and season with ground black pepper.

5 Once marinated, toss the tofu and its marinade with the broccoli, mushrooms and spring onions. Sprinkle with the pine nuts and serve immediately.

Chicory and avocado salad with tofu-dill dressing

In this fresh, crunchy salad the bitterness of the chicory is perfectly complemented by the rocket, crunchy walnuts and smooth avocado. The piquant creamy dressing of tofu and dill, with a hint of French mustard, completes this light and summery salad.

1 Toss the chicory and rocket leaves together in a bowl and then heap on to four individual serving plates. Peel, stone (pit) and slice the avocados, then toss in the lemon juice to prevent the slices from going brown.

2 Divide the avocado slices evenly among the plates, arranging them among the chicory and rocket leaves.

3 Sprinkle over the walnuts and season lightly with salt and pepper.

4 Make the dressing by blending all the ingredients except the oil in a food processor or blender. With the machine running, gradually add the oil. Taste and adjust the seasoning. Drizzle the dressing over the salad and serve immediately.

VARIATION The dressing could be made with other fresh herbs, such as coriander (cilantro), basil or parsley.

COOK'S TIP Keep any remaining dressing in the refrigerator for use on another salad, as it is very versatile.

SERVES 4

3 chicory (Belgian endive) heads, leaves separated, washed and dried
50g/2oz rocket (arugula), washed and dried
2 large ripe avocados
juice of ½ lemon
90g/3½oz/scant 1 cup walnut halves
sea salt and ground black pepper

For the dressing
15g/½oz/½ cup dill, any tough stalks removed
1 small garlic clove, crushed
juice of 1 lemon
5ml/1 tsp clear honey
5ml/1 tsp light soy sauce
350g/12oz silken tofu
5ml/1 tsp French mustard
pinch of salt
50ml/2fl oz/¼ cup olive oil

SERVES 4

600g/1lb 6oz green beans, trimmed
30ml/2 tbsp olive oil
4 shallots, finely chopped
400g/14oz cherry tomatoes, halved

For the tofu pesto
1 tomato, chopped
2 garlic cloves, coarsely chopped
30g/1¼oz fresh basil or ½ bunch of fresh parsley, any tough stems removed and the rest chopped
105ml/7 tbsp olive oil
150g/5oz silken tofu
dash of lemon juice
50g/2oz/½ cup ground almonds
sea salt and ground black pepper

Green bean and tomato salad with tofu pesto

This classic salad of green beans and sweet cherry tomatoes is combined with a silken tofu version of pesto that is creamy and delicious.

1 First make the pesto by processing the tomato and garlic in a blender or food processor until smooth. Add the rest of ingredients, season and blend again until the sauce is smooth and creamy.

2 Blanch the beans in boiling salted water for 2 minutes, or until just tender. Drain.

3 Meanwhile, heat the oil in a frying pan over a gentle heat and stir-fry the shallots for 4 minutes until softened.

4 Add the blanched beans and cherry tomatoes to the pan with the pesto. Toss together to mix well and serve hot or leave to cool, then chill to serve cold.

Spiralized vegetable salad with tofu dressing

Here a combination of sprouted beans and seeds is mixed with spiralized sweet and juicy carrot and apple. The smooth creamy tofu dressing adds extra protein to the salad.

1 If you have a spiralizer, spiralize the carrots and the apple, and cut into slightly shorter lengths. Alternatively, slice the carrots and apple thinly and then slice again into think strips. Put in a bowl, add the bean and alfalfa seed sprouts and mix together.

2 To make the dressing, put the tofu, milk, mustard, lemon juice or rice vinegar and salt and pepper in a small food processor or blender. Blend until smooth. The dressing should be thick, but still a pourable consistency, so stir in a further 15ml/1 tbsp almond or soya milk if necessary.

3 Drizzle half the dressing over the salad and mix together to lightly coat. Drizzle the rest of the dressing over the salad, then sprinkle with toasted sesame seeds. Serve straight away.

SERVES 4

2 medium carrots, peeled
1 green-skinned eating apple
115g/4oz mung beansprouts
50g/2oz sprouted alfalfa seeds
15ml/1 tbsp toasted sesame seeds

For the tofu dressing
115g/4oz silken tofu
45ml/3 tbsp almond or soya milk
1.5ml/¼ tsp Dijon mustard
5ml/1 tsp lemon juice or rice vinegar
Salt and ground black pepper

Stir-fried crispy tofu and asparagus

Asparagus is not only elegant but also delicious. This fabulous Thai dish, combining tofu and asparagus, is the perfect side dish to serve when fresh asparagus is in season.

1 Preheat the grill or broiler to medium. Place the tofu cubes in a grill pan and grill for 2–3 minutes, then turn them over and continue to cook until they are crisp and golden brown all over. Watch them carefully; they must not be allowed to burn.

2 Heat the oil in a wok or heavy frying pan. Add the green curry paste and cook over a medium heat, stirring constantly, for 1–2 minutes, until it gives off its aroma.

3 Stir the soy sauce, lime leaves, sugar and vegetable stock into the wok or pan and mix well. Bring to the boil, then reduce the heat to low so that the mixture is just simmering.

4 Add the asparagus and simmer gently for 5 minutes. Meanwhile, chop each piece of tofu into four, then add to the pan with the peanuts.

5 Toss to coat all the ingredients in the sauce, then spoon into a warmed dish and serve immediately.

VARIATION Substitute slim carrot batons, baby leeks or small broccoli florets for the asparagus, if you like.

SERVES 2

250g/9oz deep-fried tofu cubes

30ml/2 tbsp groundnut (peanut) oil

15ml/1 tbsp Thai green curry paste

30ml/2 tbsp light soy sauce

2 kaffir lime leaves, rolled into cylinders and thinly sliced

30ml/2 tbsp sugar

150ml/¼ pint/⅔ cup vegetable stock

250g/9oz asparagus, trimmed and sliced into 5cm/2in lengths

30ml/2 tbsp roasted peanuts, finely chopped

Stir-fried tofu with Chinese chive stems

SERVES 4

200g/7oz firm tofu, drained
30ml/2 tbsp groundnut
(peanut) oil
450g/1lb Chinese chives, cut
into 5cm/2in lengths
30ml/2 tbsp light soy sauce
2.5ml/½ tsp ground black
pepper
15ml/1 tbsp sesame oil

This delightfully simple dish is full of colour and flavour. The stir-fried tofu adds texture and takes on the flavour of the nutty oil beautifully. Chinese chives are quite different from common chives, being thicker and juicier, rather like green beans, and tipped with small pale-green heads.

1 Cut the tofu into four squares and again into thin slices, each about 5mm/¼in thick.

2 Heat the oil in a wok over a high heat. Add the tofu and fry for 1 minute, or until lightly browned on both sides. Do not over-stir or you will break up the pieces.

3 Push the tofu to one side, add the chives and stir-fry for 1 minute, taking care not to break up the tofu. Add the soy sauce, pepper, sesame oil and 60ml/4 tbsp water, and stir for 1 minute more, or until the water has evaporated and the chives are just tender. Serve hot.

SERVES 4

4 red (bell) peppers
1 orange (bell) pepper, seeded and coarsely chopped
1 yellow (bell) pepper, seeded and coarsely chopped
60ml/4 tbsp garlic or herb olive oil
250g/9oz firm tofu, drained
50g/2oz/½ cup pine nuts

Roasted peppers with tofu

Here is an alternative to the more usual meat- or rice-stuffed classic dish. The tofu will soften and melt into the peppers as they bake and the use of garlic or herb olive oil enhances the flavour.

1 Preheat the oven to 220°C/425°F/Gas 7. Cut the red peppers in half, leaving the stalks intact, and discard the seeds. Place the red pepper halves on a baking sheet and fill with the chopped orange and yellow peppers.

2 Drizzle with half the garlic or herb olive oil and bake for approximately 25 minutes, or until the edges of the peppers are beginning to char.

3 Using a sharp knife, cut the tofu into slices and then into 2cm/¾in cubes.

4 Remove the peppers from the oven, but leave the oven switched on. Tuck the tofu cubes in among the chopped orange and yellow peppers. Sprinkle evenly with the pine nuts and drizzle with the remaining garlic or herb oil. Bake for a further 15 minutes, or until well browned. Serve warm or at room temperature.

SERVES 4

500g/1¼lb snake beans, thinly
sliced
200g/7oz silken tofu, cut into
cubes
2 shallots, thinly sliced
200ml/7fl oz/scant 1 cup
coconut milk
115g/4oz/1 cup roasted
peanuts, chopped
juice of 1 lime
10ml/2 tsp palm sugar or light
muscovado (brown) sugar
60ml/4 tbsp light soy sauce
5ml/1 tsp dried chilli flakes

Snake beans with tofu

Here a smooth creamy tofu and coconut sauce is drizzled
over bright green beans making an attractive side dish
packed full of flavour. Another name for snake beans is yard-
long beans. Look for them in Asian stores and markets.

1 Bring a pan of lightly salted water to the boil. Add the beans
and blanch them for 30 seconds.

2 Drain the beans immediately, then refresh under cold water and
drain again, shaking well to remove as much water as possible.
Place in a serving bowl and set aside.

3 Put the tofu and shallots in a pan with the coconut milk. Heat
gently, stirring, until the tofu begins to crumble.

4 Add the peanuts, lime juice, sugar, soy sauce and chilli flakes.
Heat, stirring, until the sugar has dissolved. Pour the sauce over
the beans, toss to combine and serve immediately.

VARIATIONS The sauce also works very well with mangetouts (snow
peas). Alternatively, stir in sliced yellow or red (bell) pepper.

Fried garlic mushrooms and tofu

A simple and inexpensive recipe that can be quickly and easily prepared to make a tasty and nutritious midweek family supper. In summer, serve with mixed salad leaves or steamed greens and minted new potatoes and, in winter, serve with baked potatoes.

1 Using a sharp knife slice the tofu thinly to make 16 slices.

2 Melt one-third of the butter in a frying pan. Add the garlic and cook over a medium heat, stirring, until golden, but do not allow it to burn. Remove the garlic from the pan. Add half the remaining butter to the pan, add the mushrooms and cook for 3–4 minutes, until golden and softened, then remove the mushrooms from the pan.

3 Place the tofu in the pan with the remaining butter and cook over a medium heat. Turn over and cook the other side until golden and the tofu is warmed through.

4 Return the garlic to the pan, add the soy sauce and sake or lemon juice and simmer for 1 minute. Transfer to warm serving plates and serve immediately with the mushrooms.

SERVES 4

500g/1¼lb firm tofu, drained
50g/2oz/¼ cup butter
2 garlic cloves, thinly sliced
200g/7oz enoki or other mushrooms
45ml/3 tbsp dark soy sauce
30ml/2 tbsp sake (Japanese rice wine) or lemon juice

Marinated tofu and broccoli with crispy fried shallots

This meltingly tender tofu flavoured with a fragrant blend of spices and served with young stems of broccoli makes a perfect light supper or lunch. You can buy the crispy fried shallots from Asian supermarkets, but they are very easy to make yourself.

1 Cut the tofu into 4 triangular pieces: slice the block in half widthways, then diagonally. Place in a heatproof dish.

2 In a small bowl, combine the kecap manis, chilli sauce, soy sauce, sesame oil and ginger, then pour over the tofu. Leave the tofu to marinate for at least 30 minutes, turning occasionally.

3 Place the broccoli on a heatproof plate and place on a trivet or steamer rack in the wok. Cover and steam for 4–5 minutes, until just tender. Remove and keep warm.

4 Place the dish of tofu on the trivet or steamer rack in the wok, cover and steam for 4–5 minutes.

5 Divide the broccoli among four warmed serving plates and top each one with a piece of tofu.

6 Spoon the remaining juices over the tofu and broccoli, then sprinkle over the coriander, sesame seeds and crispy shallots and serve immediately.

COOK'S TIP Kecap manis is an Indonesian soy sauce that is slightly sweeter than normal soy sauce. It can be found in Asian stores.

SERVES 4

500g/1¼lb firm tofu, drained
45ml/3 tbsp kecap manis
30ml/2 tbsp sweet chilli sauce
45ml/3 tbsp light soy sauce
5ml/1 tsp sesame oil
5ml/1 tsp finely grated fresh root ginger
400g/14oz tenderstem broccoli, halved lengthways
45ml/3 tbsp roughly chopped coriander (cilantro)
30ml/2 tbsp toasted sesame seeds
30ml/2 tbsp crispy fried shallots

Steamed egg and tofu custard

SERVES 4

4 eggs
2.5ml/½ tsp ground white pepper
15ml/1 tbsp light soy sauce
a pinch of sugar
275g/10oz soft tofu, drained
15ml/1 tbsp sesame oil
1 spring onion (scallion), chopped
5ml/1 tsp chopped preserved winter vegetable (tung chai)

This is a delicious, light dish that is very easy to prepare. It requires only eggs and tofu: two products that have a great affinity with each other. It provides a perfect contrast to deep-fried meat and chicken dishes. The seasonings and toppings can be varied to taste, but sesame oil and pepper are recommended. Use soft or silken tofu for the best results.

1 Lightly beat the eggs (do not over-beat) and season with pepper, soy sauce and sugar.

2 In a separate bowl, mash the tofu with a fork, add the sesame oil and 45ml/3 tbsp water, then mash again until smooth.

3 Add the egg mixture and chopped spring onion to the tofu, and stir well to incorporate. Transfer to a deep plate or shallow bowl that will fit into your steamer.

4 Sprinkle the chopped winter vegetable over the top, and steam for 10 minutes, or until the custard is set.

COOK'S TIP Tung chai, or winter vegetable, is a type of pickled Chinese cabbage that is slightly salty.

VARIATION If you are not serving this to vegetarians, you can add 30ml/2 tbsp minced (ground) pork or chicken to the egg mixture and mix well. Continue with step 2, but steam for 15 minutes, until the meat is cooked through.

VEGETARIAN MAINS

The recipes in this chapter demonstrate how indispensable tofu is in the vegetarian kitchen. It plays a starring role in burgers, wraps, kebabs and stir-fries. Influences from around the world are incorporated into these recipes from Mexican tortillas to spicy tofu stir-fries and Thai vegetable curry.

90g/3½oz/½ cup brown rice
15ml/1 tbsp vegetable oil
1 onion, finely chopped
1 garlic clove, crushed
200g/7oz/1¾ cups peanuts
250g/9oz firm tofu, drained
and crumbled
small bunch of fresh coriander
(cilantro) or parsley, chopped
(optional)
30ml/2 tbsp light soy sauce
30ml/2 tbsp olive oil, for
shallow frying

Peanut and tofu cutlets

These delicious peanut and tofu patties make a filling and
nutritious midweek meal, served with lightly steamed green
vegetables or a crisp salad, and a tangy salsa or ketchup.

1 Cook the rice according to the instructions on the packet until
tender, then drain. Heat the vegetable oil in a large, heavy frying
pan and cook the onion and garlic over a low heat, stirring
occasionally, for about 5 minutes, until softened and golden.

2 Meanwhile, spread out the peanuts on a baking sheet and toast
under the grill or broiler for a few minutes, until browned. Place
the peanuts, cooked onion and garlic, rice, tofu, coriander or
parsley, if using, and soy sauce in a blender or food processor and
process until the mixture comes together in a thick paste.

3 Divide the paste into eight equal-size mounds and form each
mound into a cutlet shape or square.

4 Heat the olive oil in a large, heavy frying pan. Add the cutlets,
in two batches if necessary, and cook for 5–10 minutes on each
side, until golden and heated through. Remove from the pan with
a metal spatula and drain on kitchen paper. Keep warm while you
cook the remaining batch, then serve immediately.

Vegetable tofu burgers

These soft golden burgers are stuffed full of tasty tofu and vegetables. They are quick and easy to make and very popular with kids.

1 Cook the potatoes in salted, boiling water for 10–12 minutes, until tender, then drain. Meanwhile, cook the frozen vegetables in boiling water for 5 minutes, or until tender, then drain well.

2 Meanwhile, heat 15ml/1 tbsp of the oil in a large frying pan. Add the leeks and garlic and cook over a low heat, stirring occasionally, for about 5 minutes, until softened and golden.

3 Mash the potatoes, then add the vegetables and all the other ingredients except the oil but including the cooked leeks and garlic. Season to taste, then mix together well and divide into eight equal-size mounds.

4 Shape each mound into a burger. Heat another 15ml/1 tbsp oil in the frying pan. Cook four burgers at a time over a gentle heat for 4–5 minutes on each side, until golden brown and warmed through. Repeat with the remaining four burgers, using the remaining oil. Keep the first batch warm in a low oven. Serve in buns topped with salad leaves and slices of tomato and cucumber.

SERVES 4

4 potatoes, peeled and cubed
250g/9oz frozen mixed vegetables, such as corn, green beans, (bell) peppers
45ml/3 tbsp vegetable oil
2 leeks, coarsely chopped
1 garlic clove, crushed
250g/9oz firm tofu, drained and crumbled
30ml/2 tbsp light soy sauce
15ml/1 tbsp tomato purée (paste)
115g/4oz/2 cups fresh breadcrumbs
small bunch of fresh coriander (cilantro) or parsley (optional)
salad leaves
1 tomato, thinly sliced
½ cucumber, thinly sliced
sea salt and ground black pepper

Tofu tortillas

SERVES 4

30ml/2 tbsp olive oil
1 red (bell) pepper, seeded and finely diced
1 small red onion, finely chopped
1 garlic clove, finely chopped
250g/9oz firm tofu, drained and crumbled
400g/14oz can red kidney beans, drained and rinsed
juice of ½ lemon
15ml/1 tbsp chilli sauce or 2.5ml/½ tsp dried chilli flakes (optional)
15ml/1 tbsp light soy sauce
small bunch of fresh coriander (cilantro), chopped (optional)
8 × 18cm/7in flour tortillas
sea salt and ground black pepper
50g/2oz mature (sharp) Cheddar cheese or soya cheese, grated (optional) to serve

For the guacamole
2 ripe avocados
50g/2oz cherry tomatoes, peeled and chopped
½ shallot, finely chopped
juice of ½ lemon

A succulent, lightly spiced mixture of tofu, vegetables and kidney beans is served in tortilla wraps with grated cheese and freshly made guacamole. This is a great idea for a mid-week family supper or an informal dinner.

1 Heat the oil in a large frying pan. Add the red pepper, onion and garlic and cook over a medium heat, stirring occasionally, for about 5 minutes, until softened and golden.

2 Add the tofu, kidney beans, lemon juice, chilli sauce or chilli flakes, soy sauce and coriander and season with sea salt and pepper to taste, then heat through gently, breaking up the tofu with the back of a wooden spoon.

3 Warm the tortillas individually in a heavy frying pan or stacked in the microwave, according to the manufacturer's instructions, then spoon the filling in a line down the centre of each, top with grated cheese, if using, and roll up. Place on a serving platter or individual plates.

4 To make the guacamole, peel the avocados, remove the stones and chop the flesh. Process in a blender or food processor with the cherry tomatoes, shallot, lemon juice and seasoning. Alternatively, place in a bowl and mash with a fork.

Fried tofu and rice noodles

SERVES 4

200g/7oz cellophane noodles
8 spring onions (scallions), thinly sliced
300g/11oz marinated deep-fried tofu, cubed
about 2.5ml/½ tsp dried chilli flakes
grated rind and juice of 1 lemon
5cm/2in piece fresh root ginger, sliced into fine batons (optional)
1 bunch fresh coriander (cilantro) or parsley, chopped
30ml/2 tbsp light soy sauce
30ml/2 tbsp toasted sesame oil
65g/2½oz/½ cup sesame or sunflower seeds, toasted
salt and ground black pepper

A light and refreshing salad, this is a meal in itself. With a pack of marinated tofu, a bunch of spring onions and some fresh coriander, you can make this tasty dish in minutes.

1 Cover the noodles with boiling water, leave for 5–10 minutes, or according to the manufacturer's instructions, then drain and rinse under cold running water. Place in a large bowl.

2 Add the spring onions, tofu, chilli flakes, lemon rind and juice, ginger, if using, coriander, soy sauce, sesame oil and seeds and toss together. Check the seasoning and serve.

Tofu and pepper kebabs

SERVES 2

A simple coating of ground, dry-roasted peanuts pressed on to cubed tofu provides plenty of additional texture and colour along with the red and green peppers.

1 Grind the peanuts in a blender or food processor and transfer to a plate. Turn the tofu cubes in the ground nuts to coat.

2 Preheat the grill or broiler to medium. Halve and seed the peppers, and cut them into large chunks. Thread the chunks of pepper on to four large skewers with the tofu cubes and place on a foil-lined grill rack.

3 Grill the kebabs, turning frequently, for 10–12 minutes, or until the peppers and peanuts are beginning to brown. Transfer the kebabs to warmed plates and serve immediately with the sweet chilli dipping sauce.

50g/2oz/½ cup dry-roasted peanuts
250g/9oz firm tofu, drained and cut into bitesize cubes
2 red (bell) peppers
2 green (bell) peppers
60ml/4 tbsp sweet chilli dipping sauce

Tofu stir-fry with peanut sauce

Stir-fried vegetables are quick and easy to make into a colourful and appetizing meal. The addition of tofu adds protein and texture to the dish, which is further enhanced by the drizzled peanut sauce.

1 To make the sauce, heat the oil in a small wok or heavy pan. Stir in the garlic and chillies, stir-fry until they begin to colour, then add all the peanuts except 15ml/1 tbsp. Stir-fry for a few minutes until the natural oil from the peanuts begins to weep.

2 Add the remaining ingredients and bring to the boil. Reduce the heat and cook gently until the sauce thickens a little and specks of oil appear on the surface. Put aside.

3 Drain the mushrooms and lily buds and squeeze out any excess water. Cut the mushroom caps into strips and discard the stalks. Trim off the hard ends of the lily buds and tie a knot in the centre of each one. Put the mushrooms and lily buds aside.

4 Cut the tofu into slices. Heat 30ml/2 tbsp of the oil in a wok or heavy pan and brown the tofu on both sides. Drain on kitchen paper and cut it into strips.

5 Heat a wok or heavy pan and add the remaining oil. Stir in the onion and carrot and stir-fry for a minute. Add the pak choi stems and stir-fry for 2 minutes. Add the mushrooms, lily buds, tofu and bamboo shoots and stir-fry for a minute more. Toss in the pak choi leaves, followed by the soy sauce and sugar. Stir-fry until heated through.

6 Heat up the peanut sauce and drizzle over the vegetables in the wok, or spoon the vegetables into individual bowls and top with a little sauce. Garnish with the remaining peanuts and serve.

COOK'S TIP Tiger lily buds are the dried unopened flowers of the day lily plant. They are yellow–gold in colour and around 5cm/2in long. They have a delicate musky flavour. Also called golden needles, they can be found in Asian supermarkets.

SERVES 4–6

6 Chinese black mushrooms (dried shiitake), soaked in lukewarm water for 20 minutes
20 tiger lily buds (golden needles), soaked in lukewarm water for 20 minutes
225g/8oz firm tofu, drained
60ml/4 tbsp sesame or groundnut (peanut) oil
1 large onion, finely sliced
1 large carrot, finely sliced
300g/11oz pak choi (bok choy), the leaves separated from the stems
225g/8oz can bamboo shoots, drained and rinsed
50ml/2fl oz/¼ cup light soy sauce
10ml/2 tsp sugar

For the peanut sauce
15ml/1 tbsp groundnut (peanut) or sesame oil
2 garlic cloves, finely chopped
2 red chillies, seeded and finely chopped
90g/3½oz/generous ½ cup unsalted roasted peanuts, finely chopped
150ml/5fl oz/⅔ cup coconut milk
30ml/2 tbsp hoisin sauce
15ml/1 tbsp light soy sauce
15ml/1 tbsp sugar

Sweet-and-sour vegetables with tofu

SERVES 4

4 shallots
3 garlic cloves
30ml/2 tbsp groundnut
(peanut) oil
250g/9oz Chinese leaves
(Chinese cabbage), shredded
8 baby corn cobs, sliced
diagonally
2 red (bell) peppers, seeded
and thinly sliced
200g/7oz/1¾ cups mangetouts
(snow peas), trimmed and
sliced
250g/9oz firm tofu, drained
and cut into bitesize cubes
60ml/4 tbsp vegetable stock
30ml/2 tbsp light soy sauce
15ml/1 tbsp sugar
30ml/2 tbsp rice vinegar
2.5ml/½ tsp dried chilli flakes
small bunch of fresh coriander
(cilantro), chopped

Big, bold and beautiful, this is a hearty stir-fry that will satisfy
the hungriest guests. Stir-fries are always a good choice when
entertaining as they take a short time to cook.

1 Slice the shallots thinly using a sharp knife. Finely chop the
garlic.

2 Heat the oil in a wok or large frying pan and cook the shallots
and garlic for 2–3 minutes over a medium heat, until golden. Do
not let the garlic burn or it will taste bitter.

3 Add the shredded cabbage, toss over the heat for 30 seconds,
then add the corn cobs and repeat the process.

4 Add the red peppers, mangetouts and tofu in the same way,
each time adding a single ingredient and tossing it over the heat
for about 30 seconds before adding the next ingredient.

5 Pour in the stock and soy sauce. Mix together the sugar and
vinegar in a small bowl, stirring until the sugar has dissolved, then
add to the wok or pan. Sprinkle over the chilli flakes and
coriander, toss to mix well and serve.

Braised tofu

The ingredients in this sauce provide a range of tastes: sweet, salty, nutty and spicy, and reducing the sauce during cooking forms a sticky glaze for the tofu that is irresistible.

1 Place the tofu cubes in a pan. Add 250ml/8fl oz/1 cup cold water, the anchovy or seafood stock, soy sauce and kelp.

2 Stir in the honey and garlic, then bring to the boil. Cover and boil for 5 minutes.

3 Add the onion, chillies and chilli powder. Reduce the heat and simmer, uncovered, for a further 10 minutes, until the liquid has reduced to a small amount of sauce.

4 Transfer to a serving dish and garnish with sesame seeds.

SERVES 2–3

1 block firm tofu, drained and cut into bitesize cubes
250ml/8fl oz/1 cup anchovy or seafood stock
45ml/3 tbsp dark soy sauce
1 sheet dried kelp, chopped
15ml/1 tbsp honey
1 garlic clove, crushed
½ white onion, finely chopped
1 green chilli, seeded and sliced
1 red chilli, seeded and sliced
15ml/1 tbsp Korean chilli powder
5ml/1 tsp sesame seeds, to garnish

Salad wraps with pumpkin, tofu, peanuts and basil

SERVES 4–5

This is a fun 'do-it-yourself' dish that is perfect for an informal supper party with friends or family lunch. You place all the ingredients on the table with the rice wrappers for everyone to assemble their own wraps according to their own tastes.

1 Heat a heavy pan and smear with a little oil. Place the block of tofu in the pan and sear on both sides. Transfer to a plate and cut into thin strips.

2 Heat 30ml/2 tbsp oil in the pan and stir in the shallots and garlic. Add the pumpkin and carrot, then pour in the soy sauce and 120ml/4fl oz/½ cup water. Add a little salt to taste and cook gently until the vegetables have softened but still have a bite to them.

3 Meanwhile, arrange the tofu, chillies, lettuce, basil, roasted peanuts and hoisin sauce in separate dishes and put them on the table.

4 Fill a bowl with hot water and place it in the middle of the table, or fill a small bowl for each person, and place the stack of rice wrappers beside it. Tip the cooked vegetable mixture into a dish and add to the bowls of ingredients on the table.

5 To eat, take a rice wrapper and dip it in the water for a few seconds to soften. Lay the wrapper flat on the table or on a plate and, just off-centre, spread a few strips of lettuce, followed by the pumpkin mixture, some tofu, a sprinkling of chillies, a drizzle of hoisin sauce, some basil leaves, olives and peanuts, layering the ingredients in a neat stack. Pull the shorter edge of the wrapper (the side with filling on it) up over the stack, tuck in the sides and roll into a tight cylinder.

about 30ml/2 tbsp groundnut (peanut) or sesame oil
175g/6oz firm tofu, drained
4 shallots, halved and sliced
2 garlic cloves, finely chopped
350g/12oz pumpkin flesh, cut into strips
1 carrot, cut into strips
15ml/1 tbsp light soy sauce
3–4 green Thai chillies, seeded and finely sliced
1 small, crispy lettuce, torn into strips
1 bunch fresh basil, stalks removed
115g/4oz/⅔ cup roasted peanuts, chopped
16 black olives, stoned and halved
100ml/3½fl oz/scant ½ cup hoisin sauce
20 dried rice wrappers
salt

Vegetable and tofu cake with mustard dip

SERVES 2

300g/11oz firm tofu, drained
1 carrot, finely chopped
115g/4oz mangetouts (snow peas), sliced
3 eggs
5ml/1 tsp sake (Japanese rice wine)
10ml/2 tsp salt
5ml/1 tsp grated fresh root ginger
5ml/1 tsp sesame oil
5ml/1 tsp sesame seeds
ground black pepper
vegetable oil, for greasing

For the mustard dip
45ml/3 tbsp Dijon mustard
15ml/1 tbsp sugar syrup (see Cook's Tip)
7.5ml/1½ tsp light soy sauce
30ml/2 tbsp rice vinegar
salt

This dish is filled with a mouthwatering blend of tastes and textures, yet is simple to prepare. The contrast between the delicate texture of the tofu and the crunchiness of the mangetouts is delightful.

1 Bring a large pan of salted water to the boil. Add the block of tofu and then bring it back to the boil. Use a large fish slice or metal spatula to remove and drain the tofu from the pan.

2 Crumble the block of tofu on to a piece of muslin or cheesecloth, and then squeeze it to drain off any excess water.

3 Bring a fresh batch of water to the boil and blanch the carrot for 1 minute. Add the mangetouts, bring back to the boil and then drain the vegetables. The vegetables should be slightly cooked but retain their crunchy texture.

4 Beat the eggs and sake together briefly, then add them to the crumbled tofu. Mix in the mangetouts and carrots, salt, ginger, sesame oil and sesame seeds. Season with a little black pepper and mix well.

5 Grease a 18cm/7in mould with a little oil. Pour the mixture into the mould and place in a steamer. Lay a piece of foil over the top of the mould, to keep steam out, and steam over boiling water for 20 minutes, until the mixture is set and firm.

6 Meanwhile, for the dip, mix the mustard, syrup, soy sauce and vinegar. Season with a little salt. Mix thoroughly.

7 Slide a metal spatula or palette knife between the tofu and the mould. Cover with a serving plate and then invert mould and plate. Remove the mould and serve the tofu sliced, with the dipping sauce.

COOK'S TIP To make sugar syrup, dissolve 1 part white sugar in 2 parts water over a low heat. Stir until the sugar has dissolved, then bring to the boil for 1 minute. Remove from the heat and leave to cool. Store in the refrigerator for up to 2 weeks.

Tofu with lemon grass, basil and peanuts

This very tasty dish is a wonderful way to cook tofu. The recipe here uses basil leaves but lime, coriander or curry leaves would work equally well in this simple stir-fry. It can be served on its own with rice or with other vegetable dishes and salads, accompanied by the traditional ginger sauce nuoc mam gung. For the best results, leave the tofu to marinate for the full hour.

1 In a bowl, mix together the lemon grass, soy sauce, chillies, garlic, turmeric and sugar until the sugar has dissolved. Add a little salt to taste and add the tofu, making sure it is well coated. Leave to marinate for 1 hour.

2 To make the sauce, mix the nuoc mam with the lime juice and honey until well blended. Beat in the oil, ginger and chillies, then leave to stand for at least 30 minutes.

3 Heat a wok or heavy pan. Pour in the oil, and stir in the marinated tofu, turning it frequently to make sure it is evenly cooked. Add the peanuts and most of the basil leaves.

4 Tip the tofu on to a serving dish, scatter the remaining basil leaves over the top and serve with the nuoc mam gung.

SERVES 3–4

3 lemon grass stalks, finely chopped
45ml/3 tbsp dark soy sauce
1–2 red Serrano chillies, seeded and finely chopped
2 garlic cloves, crushed
5ml/1 tsp ground turmeric
10ml/2 tsp sugar
300g/11oz firm tofu, drained and cut into bitesize cubes
30ml/2 tbsp groundnut (peanut) oil
45ml/3 tbsp roasted peanuts, chopped
1 bunch fresh basil, stalks removed
salt

For the sauce
15ml/1 tbsp nuoc mam
juice of 1 lime
5ml/1 tsp honey
100ml/3½fl oz/scant ½ cup groundnut (peanut) or sesame oil
75g/3oz fresh root ginger, peeled and grated
2 red thai chillies, seeded and finely chopped

Spiced tofu stir-fry

Any cooked vegetable could be added to this tasty stir-fry but it is always a good idea to try to achieve a contrast in colours and textures to make the dish more interesting.

1 Mix together the ground cumin, paprika, ginger, cayenne and sugar in a bowl and season with plenty of salt and pepper.

2 Cut the tofu into cubes with a sharp knife and gently toss the cubes in the spice mixture to coat.

3 Heat half the olive oil in a wok or large, heavy frying pan. Add the tofu cubes and cook over a high heat for 3–4 minutes, turning occasionally (take care not to break up the tofu too much). Remove with a slotted spoon and set aside. Wipe out the wok or pan with kitchen paper.

4 Add the remaining oil to the wok or pan and cook the garlic and spring onions for 3 minutes. Add the remaining vegetables and cook over a medium heat for 6 minutes, or until they are beginning to soften and turn golden. Season well.

5 Return the tofu cubes to the wok or frying pan and add the pine nuts, lime juice and maple syrup. Heat through gently, stirring occasionally, for a few minutes, then transfer to warm serving bowls and serve immediately.

SERVES 4

10ml/2 tsp ground cumin
15ml/1 tbsp paprika
5ml/1 tsp ground ginger
good pinch of cayenne pepper
15ml/1 tbsp caster (superfine) sugar
275g/10oz firm tofu, drained
60ml/4 tbsp olive oil
2 garlic cloves, crushed
1 bunch of spring onions (scallions), sliced
1 red (bell) pepper, seeded and sliced
1 yellow (bell) pepper, seeded and sliced
225g/8oz/generous 3 cups brown-cap (cremini) mushrooms, halved or quartered, if necessary
1 large courgette (zucchini), sliced
115g/4oz fine green beans, halved
50g/2oz/scant ½ cup pine nuts
15ml/1 tbsp lime juice
15ml/1 tbsp maple syrup
salt and ground black pepper

Mushrooms with bean curd skins

The shiitake mushrooms used in this recipe, known as black mushrooms, are the premium variety with large fissures in their caps. These are called 'winter mushrooms' in China and are eaten for their symbolism of longevity as well as for their rich, husky flavour and meaty texture. Beancurd skins are factory-produced. The film that forms on top of boiling soya milk is lifted off and dried flat to form wrinkly sheets. The kind used here are the slightly glossy, translucent brown skins, rather than the opaque yellow-beige skins. These have a superior texture and flavour to spring roll skins.

SERVES 4

16 dried shiitake mushrooms, soaked for 1 hour in hot water
15ml/1 tbsp dark soy sauce
5ml/1 tsp garlic paste
5ml/1 tsp ginger paste
2.5ml/½ tsp salt
2.5ml/½ tsp ground white pepper
2.5ml/½ tsp sugar
5ml/1 tsp cornflour (cornstarch)
1 or 2 sheets of beancurd skin
chilli and garlic sauce, to serve

1 Drain the shiitake mushrooms, snip off and discard the stems and slice the caps as thinly as you can. Marinate the mushroom slices with the soy sauce, garlic, ginger, salt, pepper, sugar and cornflour for 10 minutes.

2 Lay a sheet of beancurd skin on a flat surface and wipe over gently with a damp cloth. (This is to prevent it from cracking and splitting.) Cut into pieces 13cm/5in square.

3 Put 15ml/1 tbsp of mushroom mixture on the edge of each square and roll up like a spring roll, tucking in the sides to seal as you go.

4 Put the rolls on a flat plate that will fit inside your steamer, and steam for 10–15 minutes. Serve with a chilli and garlic sauce.

COOK'S TIPS These beancurd skin parcels are sometimes brushed with a little lightly thickened stock after steaming, to give them a glossy, juicy finish.
• They can also be deep-fried, if they are first sealed with a cornflour and water paste. Beancurd skin crisps up almost immediately in hot oil.

Crisp-fried tofu in a tangy tomato sauce

This is a light, tasty dish. Cubes of firm tofu are first deep-fried and then tossed in a warm spicy sauce of tomatoes, chillies and ginger to create a warming delicious dish for everyday eating.

1 Heat enough oil for deep-frying in a wok or heavy pan. Fry the tofu, in batches, until crisp and golden. Remove with a slotted spoon and drain on kitchen paper.

2 Reserve 30ml/2 tbsp oil in the wok. Add the shallots, chilli, ginger and garlic and stir-fry until fragrant. Stir in the tomatoes, soy sauce and sugar. Reduce the heat and simmer for 10–15 minutes until it resembles a sauce. Stir in 105ml/ 7 tbsp water and bring to the boil.

3 Season with a little pepper and return the tofu to the pan. Mix well and simmer gently for 2–3 minutes to heat through. Garnish with mint leaves and chilli strips and serve immediately.

COOK'S TIP This recipe is delicious as a side dish or as a main dish with noodles or rice.

SERVES 4

vegetable or groundnut (peanut) oil, for deep-frying
450g/1lb firm tofu, drained and cut into bitesize cubes
4 shallots, finely sliced
1 Thai chilli, seeded and chopped
25g/1oz fresh root ginger, peeled and finely chopped
4 garlic cloves, finely chopped
6 large ripe tomatoes, skinned, seeded and finely chopped
30ml/2 tbsp light soy sauce
10ml/2 tsp sugar
mint leaves and strips of red chilli, to garnish
ground black pepper

SERVES 4–6

Tofu and green bean curry

600ml/1 pint/2½ cups canned coconut milk

15ml/1 tbsp Thai red curry paste

45ml/3 tbsp light soy sauce

10ml/2 tsp palm sugar or light muscovado (brown) sugar

225g/8oz/3¼ cups button (white) mushrooms

115g/4oz/scant 1 cup green beans

175g/6oz firm tofu, drained and cut into bitesize cubes

4 kaffir lime leaves, torn

2 fresh red chillies, seeded and sliced

fresh coriander (cilantro) leaves, to garnish

One of those versatile recipes that should be in every cook's repertoire. This quick and easy version uses green beans, but other types of vegetable work equally well.

1 Pour about one-third of the coconut milk into a wok or pan. Cook until it starts to separate and an oily sheen appears on the surface.

2 Add the red curry paste, soy sauce and sugar to the coconut milk. Mix thoroughly, then add the mushrooms. Stir and cook for 1 minute.

3 Stir in the remaining coconut milk. Bring back to the boil, then add the green beans and tofu cubes. Simmer gently for 4–5 minutes more.

4 Stir in the kaffir lime leaves and sliced red chillies. Spoon the curry into a serving dish, garnish with the coriander leaves and serve immediately.

Pock-marked tofu

Probably the best-known Sichuan export, this dish is truly entrenched in Chinese restaurants worldwide. It is quite spicy so use less chilli bean paste if you prefer a milder taste.

1 Cut the tofu into 2cm/¾in cubes. Spread out the cubes on a double layer of kitchen paper to drain for 10 minutes – this makes them less prone to crumbling later.

2 Heat the oil in a wok over a medium-high heat. Add the garlic and chilli, and fry for 40 seconds. Add the black bean sauce, sesame oil and chilli bean paste. Stir for 1 minute, then add the vegetable stock.

3 Bring to the boil, then add the tofu cubes, green pepper and peas. Cook for 2 minutes, stirring gently, so that the tofu doesn't break up.

4 Put the cornflour in a small bowl and blend with 15ml/1 tbsp water. Add to the wok, then stir until the sauce has thickened slightly. Serve immediately, garnished with spring onion slices.

SERVES 4

600g/1lb 6oz firm tofu, drained
30ml/2 tbsp groundnut (peanut) oil
15ml/1 tbsp finely chopped garlic
1 fresh red chilli, finely chopped
5ml/1 tsp black bean sauce
30ml/2 tbsp sesame oil
30ml/2 tbsp chilli bean paste (dou banjiang)
200ml/7fl oz/scant 1 cup strong vegetable stock
1 green (bell) pepper, finely diced
30ml/2 tbsp peas
5ml/1 tsp cornflour (cornstarch)
sliced spring onions (scallions), to garnish

Tofu with preserved bean curd

Many vegetarian dishes in China feature tofu prominently, using the different types such as soft, firm, fried or marinated tofu, which all have a high protein content. In this recipe preserved beancurd seasons the sauce for two other kinds of beancurd or tofu. The two types of tofu used here are deep-fried golden cubes or puffs, which have a slightly wrinkly skin, and dried bean curd skins.

1 Soak the dried vegetable according to the packet instructions until it swells up. Rinse and drain, then cut into small pieces.

2 Heat the oil in a wok and fry the ginger for 45 seconds over medium heat. Add the mashed preserved red beancurd and stir-fry for 20 seconds.

3 Add both types of tofu, the sugar, sesame oil, wine or sherry and pepper. Stir for 1 minute and add 250ml/8fl oz/1 cup water. Braise for 20 minutes over medium heat until the barest hint of sauce is left. Serve garnished with celery leaves.

COOK'S TIPS When you buy dried vegetable it will be called Sichuan cai in Mandarin or mui choy in Cantonese.
• You can buy ready-fried tofu cubes, but if you cut firm fresh tofu into 2.5cm/1in cubes and deep-fry them slowly until golden, it will have a meatier texture.

SERVES 4

75g/3oz dried vegetable
(see Cook's Tips)
15ml/1 tsp vegetable oil
25g/1oz fresh root ginger,
pounded to a paste
1 cube preserved red
beancurd (tofu ru), mashed
until smooth with a fork
12 pieces of deep-fried tofu
cubes, halved (see Cook's Tips)
8 pieces of dried bean curd
skins, halved
2.5ml/½ tsp sugar
15ml/1 tbsp sesame oil
30ml/2 tbsp Shaoxing wine
or dry sherry
2.5ml/½ tsp ground black
pepper
chopped fresh Chinese celery
leaves, to garnish

SERVES 4

350g/12oz dried or deep-fried tofu

115g/4oz canned straw mushrooms

1 leek, very dark ends cut off and discarded

15ml/1 tbsp vegetable oil

30ml/2 tbsp hoisin sauce

15ml/1 tbsp dark soy sauce

2.5ml/½ tsp ground black pepper

15ml/1 tbsp Shaoxing wine or dry sherry

2.5ml/½ tsp sugar

15ml/1 tbsp sesame oil

5ml/1 tsp cornflour (cornstarch)

plain boiled rice, to serve

Braised tofu with mushrooms

Tofu, whether fresh, fried or dried, can be braised with rich or subtle seasonings for a superb vegetarian dish. As a neutral product, tofu absorbs other flavours easily. In Chinese cuisine tofu is not regarded as a meat substitute, but with reverence for its own nutritional and chameleon-like qualities. With complementary ingredients like mushrooms and vegetables, this dish achieves banquet status.

1 If using dried tofu, cut each square into two triangles. If using deep-fried tofu cubes, you can leave them whole, as they are usually already bitesize.

2 Drain the straw mushrooms. Slice the leek diagonally into 1cm/½in wide slices. Wash in plenty of cold water to remove the soil that often clings to the insides of the white stalks. Drain thoroughly.

3 Heat the oil in a wok, add the leek, and stir-fry for 1 minute. Add the hoisin sauce, soy sauce, pepper, wine or sherry, sugar, sesame oil and 350ml/12fl oz/1½ cups water, and bring to the boil.

4 Add the tofu, and simmer for 10 minutes over medium heat. Just before serving, mix the cornflour with a little water and add to the pan. Stir until the sauce thickens a little, then serve immediately, with some plain rice.

COOK'S TIP To make your own fried tofu, buy the firm white variety and cut into cubes. Heat plenty of oil until smoking, and deep-fry the tofu, in batches, until a golden skin forms.

Potato rösti and tofu with fresh tomato and ginger sauce

Although this dish features various components, it is not difficult to make and the finished result is well worth the effort. Make sure you marinate the tofu for at least an hour to allow it to absorb the flavours of the ginger, garlic and tamari.

1 Mix together all the marinade ingredients in a shallow dish and add the tofu cubes. Spoon the marinade over the tofu and leave in the refrigerator for 1 hour, turning the tofu occasionally.

2 To make the rösti, par-boil the potatoes for 10–15 minutes, until almost tender. Drain well, leave to cool, then grate coarsely. Season to taste. Preheat the oven to 200°C/400°F/Gas 6.

3 Remove the tofu from the marinade and reserve the marinade. Spread out the tofu on a baking sheet and bake, turning the cubes occasionally for 20 minutes, until golden and crisp all over.

4 Take a quarter of the potato mixture at a time and form into four coarse patties with your hands.

5 Heat a frying pan with just enough oil to cover the base. Place the patties in the frying pan and flatten the mixture, using your hands or a spatula to form rounds about 1cm/½in thick. Cook for about 6 minutes, until golden and crisp on the undersides. Carefully turn over the rösti with a fish slice or metal spatula and cook for a further 6 minutes, until golden.

6 Meanwhile, make the sauce. Heat the olive oil in a pan, add the reserved marinade and the tomatoes and cook over a medium heat, stirring, for 2 minutes. Reduce the heat, cover and simmer gently, for 10 minutes. Press through a sieve to make a thick sauce.

7 To serve, place a rösti on each of four warmed serving plates. Arrange the tofu cubes on top, spoon over the tomato and ginger sauce and sprinkle with sesame seeds. Serve immediately, with salad leaves, if liked.

SERVES 4

425g/15oz firm tofu, drained and cut into bitesize cubes
4 large potatoes, about 900g/2lb total weight, peeled
sunflower oil, for frying
salt and ground black pepper
30ml/2 tbsp sesame seeds, toasted, to garnish

For the marinade
30ml/2 tbsp tamari or dark soy sauce
15ml/1 tbsp clear honey
2 garlic cloves, crushed
4cm/1½in piece fresh root ginger, grated
5ml/1 tsp toasted sesame oil

For the sauce
15ml/1 tbsp olive oil
8 tomatoes, halved, seeded and chopped

Twice-cooked tempeh

SERVES 4

45ml/3 tbsp vegetable oil
2 onions, finely chopped
2 garlic cloves, crushed
5ml/1 tsp fennel seeds,
crushed
2.5ml/½ tsp chilli flakes
5ml/1 tsp coriander seeds,
crushed
5ml/1 tsp cumin seeds,
crushed
1 red (bell) pepper, seeded
and finely chopped
450g/1lb tempeh, sliced
115g/4oz Cheddar cheese,
grated

For the sauce
30ml/2 tbsp tamari soy sauce
juice of ½ lemon
45ml/3 tbsp dark brown sugar
30ml/2 tbsp cider (apple cider)
vinegar
15ml/1 tbsp English (hot)
mustard
90ml/6 tbsp tomato purée
(paste)
150ml/¼ pint/⅔ cup water
2–3 dashes Tabasco (optional)
30ml/2 tbsp chopped flat
leaf parsley, plus extra
to garnish

This dish is first pan-fried and then oven-baked in a deeply flavoured sauce. Serve the tempeh with crispy mixed salad leaves and sliced tomatoes stuffed into warmed pitta breads.

1 Preheat the oven to 200°C/400°F/Gas 6. Heat 30ml/2 tbsp of the oil in a large frying pan or wok and sauté the onions, garlic and spices for 6–7 minutes, until golden and softened.

2 Add the pepper and cook for a further 1–2 minutes, until softened.

3 Whisk together all the sauce ingredients, apart from the parsley, and add to the pan. Simmer gently for 2–3 minutes to warm through. Finally, stir in the parsley.

4 Heat the remaining oil in a large frying pan and fry the tempeh for 2–3 minutes on each side, until golden and warmed through. Transfer to a large, shallow, heatproof serving dish.

5 Pour the finished sauce over the tempeh and sprinkle evenly with the grated cheese. Bake in the oven for about 10 minutes, until the cheese has melted and is bubbling. Garnish with chopped parsley and serve.

Vegetable moussaka with tofu topping

This Greek dish, traditionally made with lamb and topped with a cheese sauce, has been ingeniously adapted for vegetarians and vegans. It contains no animal products at all, but is still as rich-tasting and full of flavour as the original. The silken tofu that tops this excellent dish adds a creamy, velvety finish.

1 Preheat the grill or broiler to high and place the aubergine slices in one layer on the grill rack. Drizzle with olive oil and grill for 2–3 minutes on each side until lightly browned.

2 To make the sauce, heat the oil in a large pan and sauté the onions, garlic and carrots for 5–7 minutes, until softened. Add the remaining ingredients, bring to the boil, then simmer for 20 minutes, stirring occasionally. Season.

3 Meanwhile make the topping. Toast the ground almonds in a heavy frying pan, without any oil, for 1–2 minutes, tossing occasionally until golden. Reserve 75g/3oz/¾ cup. Tip the rest into a food processor and add the remaining ingredients. Process until smooth and combined, and adjust the seasoning.

4 Preheat the oven to 180°C/350°F/Gas 4. Spread half the vegetable tomato sauce in the base of a 35 × 23cm/14 × 9in deep-sided ovenproof dish. Arrange the aubergine slices on top and spread over the remaining sauce.

5 Add the tofu topping. Sprinkle with the reserved almonds. Bake for 20 minutes until the top is set and browned. Garnish with paprika and basil.

SERVES 8

600g/1lb 5oz aubergines (eggplant), cut into 2.5cm/1in slices
30ml/2 tbsp olive oil
50ml/3½ tbsp water
paprika and fresh basil leaves, to garnish

For the sauce
30ml/2 tbsp olive oil
2 large onions, coarsely chopped
2 garlic cloves, crushed
2 large carrots, finely chopped
4 courgettes (zucchini), sliced
200g/7oz mushrooms, sliced
2 × 400g/14oz cans chopped tomatoes
30ml/2 tbsp balsamic vinegar
5ml/1 tsp Tabasco sauce
15ml/1 tbsp clear honey
sea salt and ground black pepper

For the tofu topping
200g/7oz/1¾ cups ground almonds
350g/12oz silken tofu, drained
15ml/1 tbsp soy sauce
15ml/1 tbsp lemon juice
2.5ml/½ tsp English (hot) mustard powder

Tofu and vegetable Thai curry

SERVES 4

175g/6oz firm tofu, drained and cut into bitesize cubes
45ml/3 tbsp dark soy sauce
15ml/1 tbsp sesame oil
5ml/1 tsp chilli sauce
2.5cm/1in piece fresh root ginger, finely grated
225g/8oz cauliflower
225g/8oz broccoli
30ml/2 tbsp vegetable oil
1 onion, sliced
400ml/14fl oz/1⅔ cups coconut milk
150ml/¼ pint/⅔ cup water
1 red (bell) pepper, seeded and chopped
175g/6oz green beans, halved
115g/4oz/1½ cups shiitake or button (white) mushrooms, halved
shredded spring onions (scallions), to garnish

For the curry paste
2 fresh green chillies, seeded and chopped
1 lemon grass stalk, chopped
2.5cm/1in piece fresh galangal, chopped
2 kaffir lime leaves
10ml/2 tsp ground coriander
a few sprigs fresh coriander (cilantro), including the stalks

Traditional Thai ingredients – coconut milk, chillies, galangal, lemon grass and kaffir lime leaves – give this curry a wonderfully fragrant aroma and a rich flavour. The tofu is marinated with ginger and chilli and provides added zest and texture to this wonderful dish. For a more substantial dish serve with boiled rice.

1 Place the tofu in an ovenproof dish. Mix together the soy sauce, sesame oil, chilli sauce and ginger and pour over the tofu. Toss gently to coat all the cubes evenly, then leave to marinate for at least 4 hours or overnight if possible, turning and basting the tofu occasionally.

2 To make the curry paste, place the chopped chillies, lemon grass, galangal, kaffir lime leaves, ground coriander and fresh coriander in a food processor and process for a few seconds until well blended. Add 45ml/3 tbsp water and process to a thick paste.

3 Preheat the oven to 190°C/375°F/Gas 5. Using a large sharp knife, cut the cauliflower and broccoli into small florets and cut any stalks into thin slices.

4 Heat the vegetable oil in a frying pan, add the sliced onion and cook gently for about 8 minutes, or until soft and lightly browned. Stir in the prepared curry paste and the coconut milk. Add the water and bring to the boil.

5 Stir in the red pepper, green beans, cauliflower and broccoli. Transfer to a casserole dish, cover and place in the oven.

6 Stir the tofu and marinade, then place the dish in the top of the oven and cook for 30 minutes, then stir them into the curry with the mushrooms. Reduce the oven temperature to 180°C/350°F/Gas 4 and cook for about 15 minutes, or until the vegetables are tender. Garnish with spring onions and serve.

GRAINS, NOODLES & PASTA

Tofu is the perfect ingredient for use in stir-fries, rice and pasta dishes. It is quick and easy to prepare and mixes wonderfully with many Asian aromatics and spices. Try using it with quinoa, mooli noodles or spaghetti for a variety of international flavours.

Nasi goreng

This Indonesian classic is a popular food stall dish and is often eaten for breakfast. It is great for using up leftover rice and you can use almost any fresh vegetables you have to hand in this flexible recipe. The marinated tofu elevates this dish from a simple accompaniment to a nourishing main meal.

1 Whisk the red curry paste and soy sauce together in a bowl and crumble the tofu into it in large chunks. Set aside to marinate until required.

2 Cook the rice according to the instructions on the packet, until tender, then drain. (Don't add salt to Thai fragrant rice.) Meanwhile, heat the oil in a large, non-stick frying pan or wok and stir-fry the garlic and spring onions for 10 minutes, or until softened and golden.

3 Add the beans, tofu and peas and stir-fry for 5 minutes, breaking up the tofu with a spoon. Add the cooked rice and coconut and stir through.

4 Push everything to one side of the pan or wok, then tip the beaten eggs into the space. Stir gently until they set, like scrambled eggs.

5 Stir the eggs into the rice and other ingredients. Sprinkle with the peanuts and chopped coriander, transfer to warm serving bowls and serve immediately.

VARIATIONS Other vegetables to use in this recipe range from courgettes (zucchini), carrots, broccoli or beansprouts to mangetout (snow peas), watercress and Chinese leaves (Chinese cabbage).

SERVES 4

15ml/1 tbsp Indonesian or Thai red curry paste

60ml/4 tbsp light soy sauce

250g/9oz firm tofu, drained

250g/9oz/generous 1¼ cups Thai fragrant or basmati rice

30ml/2 tbsp groundnut (peanut) oil

2 garlic cloves, finely chopped

1 bunch of spring onions (scallions), thinly sliced diagonally

90g/3½oz green beans, thinly sliced

200g/7oz/1¾ cups frozen peas

50g/2oz/scant 1 cup desiccated (dry unsweetened shredded) coconut, toasted

3 eggs, lightly beaten

50g/2oz/½ cup peanuts, roasted and chopped

small bunch of fresh coriander (cilantro), chopped

Tofu and quinoa laksa

SERVES 4

10ml/2 tbsp vegetable oil
10ml/2 tbsp red curry paste
150g/5oz sweet potato,
peeled and cubed
125g/4¼oz/¾ cup pearl
quinoa
300ml/½ pint/1¼ cups coconut
milk
600ml/1 pint/ 2 cups water
15ml/1 tbsp tamarind paste
1 clove garlic, crushed
25g/1oz spring onions
(scallions), sliced into
5mm/¼in slices
8 mangetouts (snow peas)
4 baby corn, cut in half
200g/7oz firm tofu, drained
and cut into bitesize cubes
fresh coriander (cilantro),
chopped, and a 6cm/2½in
piece of cucumber cut into thin
matchsticks, to garnish

Laksa is a Malay/Singaporean curry of which there are many variants. This vegetarian version uses tofu, as well as crisp vegetables and fragrant spices, all served in a coconut milk base. Here the traditional noodles are substituted with pearl quinoa to create a substantial and mouthwatering lunch or supper dish. Serve with green tea to cool your senses.

1 Heat 15ml/1 tbsp oil in a large pan, then add the curry paste, sweet potato cubes and quinoa. Fry on medium heat for 3–4 minutes, until the spice fragrances and flavours are released.

2 Add the coconut milk to the pan and stir until smooth, then add the water and tamarind paste. Bring to the boil, then lower the heat and simmer for 12–14 minutes, stirring occasionally, until the quinoa is tender.

3 Drain the quinoa, cover to keep warm and set aside, reserving the curried coconut stock in a small pan. Do not leave the quinoa in the stock or it will continue to absorb the fluid and swell.

4 In a frying pan, heat the remaining oil and add the garlic, spring onions, mangetouts and baby corn. Stir-fry on high heat for 3–4 minutes, until softened but still crisp.

5 Add the tofu cubes to the frying pan and sear for a further 3 minutes, gently turning the cubes only once or twice to avoid breaking them. Reheat the coconut stock.

6 To serve, divide the tofu and vegetables and the quinoa mixture between four large warmed bowls, and pour over the hot stock. Garnish with fresh coriander leaves and cucumber matchsticks. Serve with green tea to cool your senses.

COOK'S TIPS Key to this recipe is keeping the vegetables crisp and the tofu intact to give a curry with well-defined shapes and texture.
• You can make the curry in advance so long as you separate the quinoa from the coconut stock, or it will absorb the liquid, leaving you with quinoa risotto.

Tofu and wild rice

SERVES 4

175g/6oz/scant 1 cup basmati rice

50g/2oz/generous ¼ cup wild rice

250g/9oz firm tofu, drained and cut into bitesize cubes

25g/1oz preserved lemon, finely chopped (see Cook's Tip)

20g/¾oz bunch of fresh parsley, chopped

For the dressing

1 garlic clove, crushed

10ml/2 tsp clear honey

10ml/2 tsp of the preserved lemon juice

15ml/1 tbsp balsamic vinegar

15ml/1 tbsp olive oil

1 small fresh red chilli, seeded and finely chopped

5ml/1 tsp harissa paste (optional)

sea salt and ground black pepper

The flavours in this salad are influenced by the cuisines of North Africa and the eastern Mediterranean. It goes particularly well with chargrilled vegetables such as red onions, tomatoes, courgettes and peppers.

1 Cook the basmati rice and the wild rice in separate pans until tender. The basmati will take about 10–15 minutes to cook while the wild rice will take about 45–50 minutes. Drain, rinse under cold water and drain again, then place together in a large bowl.

2 Meanwhile whisk together all the dressing ingredients in a small bowl. Add the tofu, stir to coat and leave to marinate while the rice cooks.

3 Gently fold the tofu, marinade, preserved lemon and parsley into the rice, check the seasoning and serve.

COOK'S TIP Preserved lemons, packed in salt, are available from Middle Eastern delicatessens or from large food halls and some supermarkets.

VARIATIONS Keep an eye open for rose harissa paste, which is available from the special range in some large supermarkets or from delicatessens or food halls. It is exceptionally delicious in this recipe and still fiery hot.

Noodles and rice with tofu and beansprout broth

This delicious dish is based on the Indonesian recipe Nasi Mi. The custom is to serve the noodles, rice, tofu, broth and sambal individually. Each person then spoons rice into a bowl, followed by the tofu and sambal, then a ladleful of broth, with the noodles eaten separately.

1 Heat enough oil in a wok or heavy pan for deep-frying. Add the tofu pieces and fry for 2–3 minutes, until golden brown on both sides, then drain on kitchen paper.

2 Cut the fried tofu into thin slices and pile them on a serving plate. Set aside.

3 Put the rice in a sieve or strainer, rinse under cold running water until the water runs clear, then drain. Transfer the rice to a pan and add about 600ml/1 pint/ 2½ cups water to cover the rice. Bring to the boil, then reduce the heat and simmer gently for about 15 minutes, until all the water has been absorbed. Turn off the heat, cover the pan and leave to steam for 10–15 minutes.

4 Meanwhile, make the broth. Heat the oil in a heavy pan, stir in the garlic, chillies and lemon grass and fry until fragrant.

5 Add 15ml/1 tbsp of the soy sauce to the mixture in the pan and pour in the chicken stock. Bring to the boil, then reduce the heat and simmer for 10–15 minutes.

6 Season the broth with the remaining soy sauce and pepper and stir in the beansprouts. Turn off the heat and keep warm in a covered pan over a very low heat or in a casserole in the oven.

7 Finally, prepare the noodles. Heat the oil in a wok, stir in the shallots and garlic and fry until they begin to colour. Toss in the prawns and cook for 2 minutes, then stir in the kecap manis with 15–30ml/1–2 tbsp water. Add the noodles, season and toss well.

8 Tip the rice and noodles into warmed dishes and serve with the tofu, a bowl of spring onions, chilli sambal and a bowl of the steaming hot broth, so that everyone can help themselves.

SERVES 4–6

corn or vegetable oil, for deep-frying
250g/9oz firm tofu, drained and cut into 4 rectangular pieces
225g/8oz/1⅛ cup jasmine rice

For the broth
15ml/1 tbsp palm or corn oil
2 garlic cloves, finely chopped
1–2 fresh red or green chillies, seeded and finely chopped
1 lemon grass stalk, finely chopped
45ml/3 tbsp light soy sauce
2 litres/3½ pints/8 cups chicken stock
450g/1lb fresh mung beansprouts
ground black pepper

For the noodles
30ml/2 tbsp palm or corn oil
4 shallots, finely sliced
2 garlic cloves, finely chopped
450g/1lb peeled cooked prawns (shrimp)
30ml/2 tbsp kecap manis (sweet soy sauce)
225g/8oz dried egg noodles, soaked in warm water for 5 minutes until softened

To serve
4–6 spring onions (scallions), finely sliced
chilli sambal

Tofu with spiralized mooli noodles

SERVES 4

6 spring onions (scallions)
15g/½oz fresh coriander (cilantro) stalks, plus extra leaves to garnish
3 thin slices fresh root ginger
1 star anise
1.2 litres/2 pints/5 cups vegetable stock
30ml/2 tbsp miso paste
4 small eggs, at room temperature
1 large mooli (daikon)
15–30ml/1–2 tbsp dark soy sauce
350g/12oz firm tofu, drained and cut into bitesize pieces
1 fresh red chilli, seeded and shredded (optional)

Although a classic tofu and noodle soup usually features wheat noodles, in this version vegetable noodles are used instead, to make a lighter, fresher dish.

1 Cut the coarse green tops off the spring onions, then slice the rest finely on the diagonal and put to one side. Place the green tops in a large pan with the coriander stalks, fresh root ginger, star anise and vegetable stock.

2 Heat gently until boiling, then lower the heat and simmer for 10 minutes. Strain, reserving the stock. Blend half a ladleful of the hot stock with the miso paste in a small bowl and set aside. Return the stock to the pan and reheat until simmering.

3 Meanwhile, bring a pan of water to the boil and lower the eggs on a spoon into the simmering water. Heat the water until bubbling gently, then cook the eggs for 5–6 minutes. Remove the eggs and place in a bowl of cold water. When the eggs are just cool enough to handle, remove the shells and cut each egg in half lengthways; the whites should be very firm, but the yolks still slightly soft.

4 While the stock and eggs are cooking, spiralize the mooli using the thin, spaghetti-sized noodle blade (if you have a spiralizer), or cut into thin strips with a sharp knife. When the stock and eggs are ready, add the mooli noodles to the simmering stock, bring back to the boil and cook for 2 minutes or until just tender. Remove the mooli noodles and divide between warmed soup bowls, pushing the noodles to one side of the bowls.

5 Stir in the reserved stock and miso mixture into the rest of the stock, with soy sauce to taste. Add the tofu and quickly heat until warmed through. Leaving the stock on the heat, remove the tofu with a slotted spoon and divide the tofu between the bowls, placing next to the noodles.

6 Add the spring onions and red chilli, if using, to the stock, then ladle over the noodles and tofu. Arrange two egg halves on top of each and serve straight away, garnished with chopped fresh coriander leaves.

Teriyaki soba noodles with tofu and asparagus

Japanese soba noodles are made from buckwheat flour, which gives them a unique texture and colour. Here they are combined with tofu and asparagus and flavoured with a home-made teriyaki sauce.

1 Cook the noodles according to the instructions on the packet, then drain and rinse under cold running water. Set aside until required.

2 Heat the sesame oil in a griddle pan or on a baking tray placed under the grill or broiler until very hot. Turn down the heat to medium, then cook the asparagus for 8–10 minutes, turning frequently, until tender and lightly browned. Set aside.

3 Meanwhile, heat the groundnut oil in a wok or large frying pan until very hot. Add the block of tofu and cook for 8–10 minutes until golden, turning it occasionally to crisp all sides. Carefully remove from the wok or pan and leave to drain on kitchen paper. Cut the tofu into 1cm/½in slices.

4 To prepare the teriyaki sauce, mix the soy sauce, sake or dry sherry, mirin and sugar together, then heat the mixture in the wok or frying pan.

5 Toss in the noodles and stir to coat them in the sauce. Heat through for 1–2 minutes, then spoon into warmed individual serving bowls with the tofu slices and asparagus. Sprinkle the spring onions and carrot on top and then sprinkle with the chilli flakes and sesame seeds. Serve immediately.

COOK'S TIP Sesame seeds are an excellent source of the antioxidant vitamin E, which acts as a natural preservative, preventing oxidation and strengthening the heart and nerves.

VARIATION Use dried egg or rice noodles instead of soba noodles, if you like.

SERVES 4

350g/12oz soba noodles
30ml/2 tbsp toasted sesame oil
½ bunch asparagus tips
30ml/2 tbsp groundnut (peanut) oil
250g/9oz firm tofu, drained
2 spring onions (scallions), cut diagonally
1 carrot, cut into thin batons
2.5ml/½ tsp chilli flakes
15ml/1 tbsp sesame seeds
salt and ground black pepper

For the teriyaki sauce
60ml/4 tbsp dark soy sauce
60ml/4 tbsp sake (Japanese rice wine) or dry sherry
60ml/4 tbsp mirin (sweet rice wine)
5ml/1 tsp sugar

Indian mee goreng

SERVES 4–6

450g/1lb fresh yellow egg noodles

115g/4oz marinated deep-fried tofu cubes

60–90ml/4–6 tbsp vegetable oil

2 eggs

30ml/2 tbsp water

1 onion, sliced

1 garlic clove, crushed

15ml/1 tbsp light soy sauce

30–45ml/2–3 tbsp tomato ketchup

15ml/1 tbsp chilli sauce

1 large cooked potato, diced

4 spring onions (scallions), shredded

1–2 fresh chillies, seeded and thinly sliced (optional)

This is a truly international recipe that combines Indian, Chinese and Western ingredients into one flavoursome dish. It is a delicious treat for lunch or supper, and quick and easy to prepare too.

1 Bring a large pan of water to the boil, add the fresh egg noodles and cook for just 2 minutes. Drain the noodles and immediately rinse them under cold water to halt any further cooking. Drain again and set aside.

2 Cut each cube of fried tofu in half with a sharp knife, refresh it in a pan of boiling water, then drain well. Heat 30ml/2 tbsp of the vegetable oil in a large, heavy frying pan.

3 Beat the eggs with the water and seasoning. Add to the pan and cook, until set. Flip over, cook the other side, then slide it out of the pan and roll up.

4 Heat the remaining oil in a large wok and stir-fry the onion and garlic for 2–3 minutes. Add the noodles, soy sauce, ketchup and chilli sauce. Toss over a medium heat for 2 minutes, then add the diced potato.

5 Reserve a few spring onions for the garnish and stir the rest into the noodles with the chilli, if using, and the tofu. Thinly slice the omelette and stir into the mixture. Serve on a hot platter garnished with spring onions.

VARIATION You can use plain firm tofu instead of deep-fried tofu. Cut it into cubes and fry until brown, then lift out with a slotted spoon.

Crispy fried tempeh and noodles

Often cooked at street stalls, this fermented tofu can be served as a snack or as part of a selection of Indonesian dishes. For a more substantial dish it is served here with stir-fried noodles. You could also accompany with a selection of pickled vegetables.

1 Heat 30ml/2 tbsp of the oil in a wok or large, heavy frying pan. Add the tempeh and stir-fry until golden brown.

2 Using a slotted spoon, transfer the fried tempeh pieces to crumpled kitchen paper to drain.

3 Wipe the wok or frying pan clean with kitchen paper.

4 Heat the remaining 15ml/1 tbsp oil in the wok or pan, stir in the shallots, garlic, galangal and chillies and fry until fragrant and beginning to colour.

5 Stir in the kecap manis and toss in the fried tempeh. Stir-fry until the sauce has reduced and clings to the tempeh.

6 Tip the tempeh on to a serving dish and sprinkle with the peanuts and coriander leaves. Serve hot with stir-fried noodles.

COOK'S TIP Kecap manis can be bought from Chinese and South-east Asian supermarkets. If you are unable to buy it, then light soy sauce can be used as an alternative.

SERVES 3–4

45ml/3 tbsp coconut
or groundnut (peanut) oil
500g/1¼lb tempeh, cut into
bitesize strips
4 shallots, finely chopped
4 garlic cloves, finely chopped
25g/1oz fresh galangal or
fresh root ginger, finely
chopped
3–4 fresh red chillies, seeded
and finely chopped
150ml/¼ pint/⅔ cup kecap
manis (Indonesian sweet soy
sauce)
30ml/2 tbsp unsalted peanuts,
crushed
1 small bunch fresh coriander
(cilantro) leaves
stir-fried noodles

Rice noodles with bean curd skins

SERVES 4

12 dried shiitake mushrooms
40g/1½oz tiger lily buds
(golden needles)
6 pieces sweet bean curd skins
vegetable oil, for deep-frying
200g/7oz rice vermicelli
30ml/2 tbsp vegetable oil,
plus extra for drizzling
3 garlic cloves, finely chopped
175g/6oz Chinese leaves
(Chinese cabbage), sliced
thinly
15ml/1 tbsp dark soy sauce
2.5ml/½ tsp salt, or to taste

This is not an overly seasoned dish but rather a light and fresh-tasting dish that is perfect for a lunch or a midweek supper. The bean curd skins add colour and a crisp texture to this simple noodle recipe.

1 Soak the shiitake mushrooms in warm water for 1 hour, until softened. Strain and reserve the soaking water and top it up to make 300ml/½ pint/1¼ cups. Snip off and discard the mushroom stems and slice the caps thinly.

2 Soak the tiger lily buds in tepid water for 20 minutes, or until softened, then drain well. Snip off any hard tips. Wipe the bean curd skins with a clean damp cloth. Cut them into 1cm/½in wide strips with kitchen scissors.

3 Heat the oil for deep-frying in a wok over medium heat or in a deep-fryer, and deep-fry the bean curd skins until crisp. Drain on kitchen paper and set aside.

4 Soak the vermicelli in hot water for about 20 minutes or until they are soft and not brittle. Drain thoroughly and drizzle a little oil all over to prevent sticking.

5 Heat the oil in a wok over high heat. Add the garlic and fry for 20 seconds, until fragrant, then add the sliced mushrooms and lily buds. Fry for 1 minute, then add the Chinese leaves and fry 1 minute more.

6 Add the vermicelli, and stir-fry for 1 minute, then add two-thirds of the reserved mushroom liquor, the soy sauce and salt. Fry vigorously until the noodles are tender, sprinkling over the remaining mushroom water if they get too dry before they are cooked. Serve, sprinkled with fried bean curd skin strips.

Vegetable and marinated tofu pasta

This vegetarian tofu pasta recipe is endlessly versatile. Feel inspired to change it to suit the ingredients you have to hand – the more colourful, the better. Make sure that you chop all the vegetables into even-size pieces so that they all cook in the same time.

1 Preheat the oven to 220°C/425°F/Gas 7. Place the carrots, butternut squash, courgettes, onion wedges and pepper in a large, deep roasting pan, spreading them out well. Add the garlic, cut side down, and herb sprigs. Drizzle over the olive oil, balsamic vinegar and soy sauce.

2 Season to taste with sea salt and pepper and toss to mix together and coat evenly with the oil. Roast the vegetables for 50–60 minutes, until they are tender and lightly browned at the edges. Toss the vegetables around once or twice during the cooking to expose different sides and cook evenly.

3 Add the tofu and cherry tomatoes to the roasting pan 10 minutes before the end of the roasting time. Meanwhile, bring a large pan of lightly salted water to the boil, add the pasta, bring back to the boil and cook for 10 minutes or until *al dente*. Drain the pasta and return to the pan with a few tablespoons of the cooking water.

4 Remove the roasting pan from the oven and squeeze the garlic out of the baked skins using a wooden spoon. Toss the pasta with the vegetables, tofu and garlic, taste and adjust the seasoning, if necessary, and serve immediately.

COOK'S TIP When cooking pasta, start timing as soon as the water returns to the boil – and boil fairly vigorously, don't simmer. Test shortly before the end of the cooking time by biting a small piece of pasta between your front teeth. It should feel tender, but still firm to the bite – *al dente*, meaning "to the tooth".

VARIATIONS Other vegetables that are lovely roasted include beetroot and celeriac.

SERVES 4

4 carrots, halved lengthways and thinly sliced diagonally
1 butternut squash, peeled, seeded and cut into small chunks
2 courgettes (zucchini), thinly sliced diagonally
1 red onion, cut into wedges
1 red (bell) pepper, seeded and sliced into thick strips
1 garlic bulb, cut in half horizontally
leaves from 4 fresh rosemary or thyme sprigs (optional)
60ml/4 tbsp olive oil
60ml/4 tbsp balsamic vinegar
30ml/2 tbsp light soy sauce
500g/1¼lb marinated deep-fried tofu cubes
10–12 cherry tomatoes, halved
250g/9oz dried pasta, such as papardelle, fusilli or conchiglie
sea salt and ground black pepper

Tofu balls with spaghetti

SERVES 4

250g/9oz firm tofu, drained and torn into rough pieces
1 onion, coarsely grated
2 garlic cloves, crushed
5ml/1 tsp Dijon mustard
15ml/1 tbsp ground cumin
1 bunch of parsley, chopped
15ml/1 tbsp light soy sauce
50g/2oz/½ cup ground almonds
30ml/2 tbsp olive oil
350g/12oz spaghetti
1 bunch of fresh basil
sea salt and ground black pepper

For the sauce
15ml/1 tbsp olive oil
1 large onion, finely chopped
2 garlic cloves, chopped
1 large aubergine (eggplant), diced
2 courgettes (zucchini), diced
1 red (bell) pepper, seeded and finely chopped
pinch of sugar
400g/14oz can chopped tomatoes
200ml/7fl oz/scant 1 cup vegetable stock

This dish makes a great family supper, as children and adults alike really love the little tofu balls and the rich vegetable sauce, while pasta never fails to please.

1 Place the drained tofu, grated onion, crushed garlic, mustard, ground cumin, chopped parsley, soy sauce and ground almonds into a bowl. Season well with sea salt and ground black pepper and mix thoroughly. Roll into about 20 walnut-sized balls, squashing the mixture together with your hands.

2 Heat the olive oil in a large frying pan, then cook the balls, turning them gently until brown all over. Remove from the pan and set aside on a plate.

3 Heat the oil for the sauce in the same frying pan, add the onion and garlic and cook for 5 minutes, or until softened.

4 Add the aubergine, courgette, pepper, sugar and seasoning and stir-fry for 10 minutes until the vegetables are beginning to soften and brown.

5 Stir in the tomatoes and stock. Cover and simmer for 20–30 minutes, or until the sauce is rich and thickened. Just before the end of the cooking time, place the tofu balls gently on top of the sauce, replace the lid and heat through for 2–3 minutes.

6 Meanwhile, cook the pasta in large pan of salted, boiling water according to the manufacturer's instructions, then drain. Sprinkle the tofu balls and sauce with the basil and check the seasoning before serving with the spaghetti.

COOK'S TIP This vegetable sauce will stand on its own as a sauce for meat or fish or as a filling for baked potatoes.

MEAT & FISH MAINS

This chapter will convince you that tofu is not just for vegetarians. Combining tofu with meat, poultry and seafood gives you the best of both worlds – all your favourite flavours but with far less fat. Tofu provides a delicious contrast to the other ingredients, whether it's cooked with the meat, poultry or fish, or incorporated in a creamy sauce.

Soya bean paste stew

This rich Chinese stew is a really thick and hearty casserole. The slow cooking imparts a deep, complex flavour full of spiciness. It is a satisfyingly warm dish, ideal for cold evenings, and goes particularly well with the flavour of flame-grilled meat.

1 Thickly slice the courgette, and then cut the slices into quarters.

2 In a casserole dish or heavy pan, heat the sesame oil over a high heat. Add the beef and soya bean paste to the pan, and cook until golden brown. Then add the onion and garlic to the pan and sauté gently. Add the fish stock and bring to the boil.

3 Next add the chilli and courgette slices and boil for 5 minutes. Add the tofu and mushrooms and boil for a further 2 minutes. Reduce the heat and simmer the stew gently for 15 minutes.

4 Garnish with sliced spring onion and a drizzle of sesame oil, and serve.

COOK'S TIPS When making fish stock, you can use stock (bouillon) cubes for convenience, but to make a quick alternative fish stock from scratch, simply simmer a handful of dried anchovies in 1 litre/1¾ pints/ 4 cups water for 30 minutes, and then strain the stock into a jug or pitcher.
• Enoki mushrooms are sometimes found in supermarkets under the name of snow puff mushrooms.

SERVES 2

½ courgette (zucchini)
25g/1oz enoki mushrooms
15ml/1 tbsp sesame oil, plus extra for drizzling
50g/2oz beef, finely chopped
30ml/2 tbsp soya bean paste
½ onion, finely chopped
10ml/2 tsp finely chopped garlic
550ml/18fl oz/2½ cups fish stock
1 red chilli, seeded and sliced diagonally
175g/6oz firm tofu, drained and cut into bitesize cubes
1 spring onion (scallion), sliced, to garnish

Tofu and minced pork soup

SERVES 4

250g/9oz/generous 1 cup
minced (ground) pork
5ml/1 tsp cornflour
(cornstarch)
2.5ml/½ tsp ground black
pepper
30ml/2 tbsp light soy sauce
30ml/2 tbsp sesame oil
250g/9oz firm tofu, drained
and cut into bitesize cubes
2 eggs
1 spring onion (scallion), finely
sliced on the diagonal, and
5ml/1 tsp preserved winter
vegetable (tung chai), to
garnish

This classic blend of ingredients makes a style of soup that is
popular throughout China. In Henan, Hunan and Sichuan, this
soup is cooked with various seasonings, and some will be
thickened with cornflour whereas others are enriched with
wine. The Sichuan version is usually fiery with chopped
chillies. It is a dish that allows a chef to use his ingenuity.

1 Mix the minced pork with the cornflour and pepper. Bring
800ml/27fl oz/scant 3¼ cups water to the boil in a large pan and
add the soy sauce and sesame oil.

2 Add the tofu cubes and pork, stirring vigorously with a pair of
chopsticks to separate the pork so that it does not form uneven
lumps. Simmer for 5 minutes.

3 When the pork is properly distributed, beat the eggs lightly
and add to the soup, stirring. Cook for 5 minutes, or until the
soup is thick and the egg is well incorporated. You might get
streaks of egg here and there, but this is perfectly normal.

4 Garnish with spring onion and winter vegetable, and serve in
individual bowls.

VARIATION If you like, you can garnish with fried garlic or shallots to
give the soup a crispy and aromatic edge.

SERVES 4

250g/9oz firm tofu, drained
150g/5oz/1¼ cups minced
(ground) pork
½ onion, finely chopped
10ml/2 tsp English (hot)
mustard
5ml/1 tsp finely chopped fresh
thyme or sage
plain (all-purpose) flour, for
coating
2 eggs, beaten
90g/3½oz/1¾ cups fresh
breadcrumbs
vegetable oil, for deep-frying
sea salt and ground black
pepper
sweet chilli sauce or tomato
ketchup, to serve (optional)

Pork and tofu croquettes

Combining pork and tofu in these tasty, deep-fried croquettes not only helps to eke out the meat, but also minimizes the quantity of saturated fat – resulting in an economical and healthy dish.

1 Place the tofu in a bowl and mash with a fork.

2 Heat a little vegetable oil in a large frying pan, then add the pork, onion, mustard, thyme or sage and seasoning. Stir fry for 5–10 minutes, until the pork is cooked and golden.

3 Add the pork mixture to the tofu and divide into eight equal-size portions.

4 Shape each portion into a croquette shape, then coat first in flour, then egg and, finally, breadcrumbs.

5 Heat the oil for deep-frying to 180–190°C/350–375°F or until a cube of day-old bread browns in 30 seconds. Deep-fry the croquettes until golden, then drain on kitchen paper. Serve with sweet chilli sauce or ketchup, if you like.

Thai curry with chicken and tofu

This delicious Thai curry is highly flavoured and hot. Serve with plain rice and either some steamed green beans or broccoli, or pak choi with a sprinkling of soy sauce. The combination of chicken and tofu ensure a low-fat, yet filling dish.

1 Heat the oil in a non-stick wok or large frying pan, then stir-fry the garlic, onion and ginger for 4–5 minutes, until golden brown and softened.

2 Add the chicken pieces and stir-fry for 2–3 minutes, until browned all over. Add the curry paste and stir to coat the chicken. Add the soy sauce, tofu, grated lime rind and juice, the stock and sugar, and stir-fry for 2 minutes.

3 Add the watercress and coriander, reserving a little for the garnish, and stir-fry for a further 2 minutes. Add the coconut milk and heat through gently, stirring occasionally, but do not allow to come to the boil.

4 Taste and adjust the seasoning, if necessary, then serve garnished with the peanuts and reserved coriander.

COOK'S TIP Thai curry paste is very hot, so if you haven't used it before – beware. Most people find 5ml/1 tsp enough to give the fragrant flavours without too much heat but if you are used to hot food, then increase the amount to 10ml/2 tsp. Both red and green curry pastes – made with red and green chillies respectively – are available from most supermarkets and from Asian food stores.

VARIATION Vary the vegetables used to suit the season and your taste – mangetouts (snow peas), baby corn, courgettes (zucchini), carrots, broccoli florets and green beans all work well.

SERVES 4

30ml/2 tbsp groundnut (peanut) or soya oil
2 garlic cloves, crushed
2 onions, chopped
2.5cm/1in piece fresh root ginger, finely chopped
4 skinless chicken fillets, each weighing about 150g/5oz, chopped into bitesize pieces
15–30ml/1–2 tbsp Thai green or red curry paste (see Cook's Tip)
45ml/3 tbsp light soy sauce
150g/5oz marinated deep-fried tofu
grated rind and juice of 1 lime
120ml/4fl oz/½ cup chicken stock
pinch of sugar
90g/3½oz watercress
20g/¾oz fresh coriander (cilantro), chopped
400ml/14fl oz/1⅔ cups coconut milk
30ml/2 tbsp peanuts, toasted and chopped, to garnish

SERVES 6

675g/1½lb small clams
2 × 400ml/14fl oz cans coconut milk
50g/2oz ikan bilis (dried anchovies)
900ml/1½ pints/3¾ cups water
115g/4oz shallots, finely chopped
4 garlic cloves, chopped
6 macadamia nuts or blanched almonds, chopped
3 lemon grass stalks, root trimmed
90ml/6 tbsp sunflower oil
1cm/½in cube shrimp paste
25g/1oz/2 tbsp mild curry powder
a few curry leaves
2–3 aubergines (eggplant), total weight about 675g/1½lb, trimmed
675g/1½lb peeled raw prawns (shrimp)
10ml/2 tsp sugar
1 head Chinese leaves (Chinese cabbage), thinly sliced
115g/4oz/2 cups beansprouts, rinsed
2 spring onions (scallions), finely chopped
50g/2oz crispy fried onions
115g/4oz deep-fried tofu
675g/1½lb mixed noodles (laksa, mee and behoon) or one type only
prawn (shrimp) crackers, to serve

Tofu laksa

This spicy soup, with deep-fried tofu, is marvellous party food. Guests spoon noodles into wide soup bowls, add accompaniments of their choice and enjoy with crackers.

1 Scrub the clams under cold running water and then put them in a large pan with 1cm/½in water. Bring to the boil, cover and steam for about 3–4 minutes, until all the clams have opened. Drain and discard any that remain shut. Make up the coconut milk to 1.2 litres/2 pints/5 cups with water. Put the ikan bilis in a pan and add the water. Bring to the boil and simmer for 20 minutes.

2 Meanwhile, put the shallots, garlic and nuts into a mortar. Cut off the lower 5cm/2in of two of the lemon grass stalks, chop finely and add to the mortar. Pound the mixture to a paste.

3 Heat the oil in a large pan, add the shallot paste and cook, stirring constantly, for 1–2 minutes, until the mixture gives off a rich aroma. Add the remaining lemon grass stalk. Mix the shrimp paste and curry powder to a paste with a little of the coconut milk, add to the pan and gently heat for 1 minute, stirring constantly. Stir in the remaining coconut milk and curry leaves and leave to simmer while you prepare the accompaniments.

4 Strain the ikan bilis anchovy stock into a pan, bring to the boil, then add the aubergines. Cook for about 10 minutes. Lift out of the stock, peel and cut into thick strips. Arrange the aubergines on a serving platter. Sprinkle the prawns with sugar, add to the stock and cook for 2–4 minutes, until they have just turned pink. Remove with a slotted spoon and place next to the aubergines. Add the Chinese leaves, beansprouts, spring onions and crispy fried onions to the platter, together with the clams.

5 Gradually stir the remaining stock into the pan of soup and bring to the boil. Rinse the fried tofu in boiling water, cool slightly and squeeze to remove excess oil. Cut each piece in half and add to the soup. Lower the heat to a very gentle simmer.

6 Cook the noodles, drain and pile in a dish. Remove the curry leaves and lemon grass from the soup and discard. Serve the noodles, soup and the platter of seafood and vegetables on the table, along with a bowl of prawn crackers..

Mongolian seafood and tofu steamboat

Probably one of the oldest forms of social entertainment, a Mongolian steamboat is a really festive winter warmer, a convivial repast meant for at least six people, all seated around the bubbling centrepiece. The traditional utensil is a large brass pan with a built-in funnel in the centre; charcoal is put in the space directly under the funnel and lit. Stock is then poured into the moat and, when it boils, diners immerse the foods of their choice to cook in the stock using wire mesh spoons. Today, steamboats may be charcoal or electric with a thermostatic control.

1 Preheat the steamboat and fill the moat with boiling water. Add the stock cubes. Have a kettle standing by with more water for topping up as the meal goes on.

2 While the stock is simmering, arrange all the seasonings and the main ingredients in plates and bowls set around the steamboat. Provide a wire mesh spoon, a porcelain soup spoon, chopsticks and a soup bowl for each person. (These are all available in Chinese stores.)

3 To cook and eat, each person puts a few pieces of selected raw foods into their wire mesh spoon and dunks it into the boiling stock until cooked, then they transfer it to their individual soup bowl and add seasonings, dips and garnishes to their liking.

4 When all the ingredients are eaten, the stock will be extremely rich. It can then be ladled into each bowl to drink with a spoon.

COOK'S TIPS Stock cubes are handy, but for better flavour, make your own stock.
• The selection of ingredients is entirely personal and there is no set formula. Meat, seafood, poultry, vegetables – anything you fancy can be used as a steamboat ingredient.

SERVES 8–10

2 litres/3½ pints/9 cups boiling water (plus extra on the boil)
2 meat stock (bouillon) cubes

For the seasonings, dips and garnishes
a small bottle of light soy sauce
Chinese wine or sherry
6 garlic cloves, ground and fried until golden brown
6 spring onions (scallions), chopped
3–4 small dishes of chilli sauce
3–4 small dishes of black vinegar
ground black pepper

For the steamboat ingredients
250g/9oz firm tofu, drained and cut into bitesize cubes
450g/1lb chicken breast, thinly sliced
450g/1lb peeled raw prawns (shrimp)
30 prepared fish balls
4 pieces of fish cake
100g/3¾oz mung bean noodles, soaked
1 large Chinese cabbage, sliced into small pieces
50g/2oz tiger lily buds (golden needles), soaked and trimmed
200g/7oz pig's liver, thinly sliced

Braised tofu with crab

SERVES 4

450g/1lb firm tofu, drained and cut into bitesize cubes
vegetable oil, for deep-frying
15ml/1 tbsp vegetable oil
2 garlic cloves, chopped
30ml/2 tbsp rice wine
15m/1 tbsp yellow bean sauce
15ml/1 tbsp hoisin sauce
75g/3oz bamboo pith, soaked until soft
1 egg, lightly beaten
350g/12oz white crab meat
1 red chilli, finely chopped, to garnish

This delicate dish of crab and tofu is made from a range of contrasting flavours. It uses dried bamboo pith, which, when cooked, imparts a crunchy texture in contrast to the soft tofu and crab meat. The seasonings are a subtle mixture of yellow bean sauce, wine and hoisin sauce. If you do not have time to prepare fresh crab, use good quality canned crab meat.

1 Heat the oil in a wok or deep-fryer until smoking, then lower the tofu pieces into the oil, one at a time, and deep-fry until a brown skin forms. Lift out with a slotted spoon and set aside.

2 Heat 15ml/1 tbsp oil in a large pan and fry the garlic for 20 seconds. Add the rice wine, yellow bean sauce and hoisin sauce, and stir for 30 seconds.

3 Cut the bamboo pith into short lengths about 4cm/1½in wide. Add to the pan with 350ml/12fl oz/1½ cups water and simmer for 3 minutes. Add the tofu and lightly beaten egg, and stir for 1 minute, or until the sauce is slightly thick.

4 Add the crab meat and stir for 30 seconds to heat through. Serve hot, garnished with the chilli.

COOK'S TIPS Scallops can also be cooked in the same way. Use frozen or fresh from the shell.
• If bamboo pith is not available, use ordinary canned bamboo shoots.

Seafood and tofu paella

Not exactly authentic, but given that there are as many versions of paella as there are cooks in Spain, why not enjoy an easy and inexpensive tofu version of this tasty dish?

1 Place the saffron in a small bowl and add the boiling water. Set aside to soak for 5 minutes.

2 Heat the oil in a large, non-stick frying pan or wok, add the garlic and red pepper and stir-fry over a medium heat for 6–8 minutes, or until the garlic is golden and the pepper softened.

3 Add the tomatoes, saffron and its soaking water, paprika or cayenne pepper, thyme, rice, wine, stock, grated lemon rind and juice and bay leaf and season to taste with salt and pepper. Stir together to mix well. Bring to the boil, lower the heat, cover and simmer gently, for 10 minutes.

4 Meanwhile, using a sharp knife, slice the courgettes or patty pan squashes on the diagonal into even-size pieces about 3mm/⅛in thick.

5 Stir the rice mixture, then pile the courgettes or patty pan squashes, peas, spring onions, seafood and tofu on top of it. Replace the lid and cook for 10 minutes, then uncover and gently fold together, scraping any crusty residue from the base of the pan or wok.

6 Taste and adjust the seasoning, if necessary, and serve immediately with lemon wedges, if you like.

VARIATIONS Leave out the seafood and add more summer vegetables, such as green beans, or broad (fava) beans, and use vegetable stock instead of chicken for a vegan dish.
• Substitute skinless, boneless chicken breast portions or thighs for the seafood. Dice the meat and stir-fry with the garlic and red (bell) pepper in step 2.

SERVES 4

pinch of saffron threads
30ml/2 tbsp boiling water
15ml/1 tbsp vegetable oil
1 garlic clove, crushed
1 red (bell) pepper, seeded and diced
2–3 ripe tomatoes, coarsely chopped
1.5ml/¼ tsp paprika or cayenne pepper
10g/¼oz thyme, woody stems removed, the rest chopped
200g/7oz/1 cup long grain or basmati rice
50ml/2fl oz/¼ cup dry white wine
600ml/1 pint/2½ cups chicken stock
grated rind and juice of ½ lemon
1 bay leaf
225g/8oz small courgettes (zucchini) or patty pan squashes
150g/5oz/1¼ cups fresh or frozen peas
1 bunch of spring onions (scallions), chopped
225g/8oz cooked frozen seafood
250g/9oz firm tofu, drained and cut into bitesize pieces
sea salt and ground black pepper
lemon wedges, to serve (optional)

Tofu fish in a spicy sauce

Texture is fundamental to Chinese cuisine, and is often described as kou kan, which is loosely translated as 'mouth feel'. In this dish, kou kan is highlighted in the contrasting textures of soft tofu with the crispness of the fried fish combined in a hot chilli sauce.

1 Cut the fish into 2.5cm/1in cubes. Heat 60ml/4 tbsp oil in a wok over a high heat. When very hot, add the tofu cubes and fry, turning frequently, until well browned. Lift out using a slotted spoon and drain on kitchen paper.

2 Reduce the heat to medium and add the fish to the remaining oil. Fry for 4 minutes, gently turning the cubes a few times, until they are lightly browned all over and almost cooked through. Transfer to a plate and set aside.

3 Wipe the wok using kitchen paper and add the remaining oil. Add the garlic and fry for 1 minute, then add yellow bean sauce, soy sauce, chillies and sugar, and fry for 1 minute.

4 Add 150ml/¼ pint/⅔ cup water and simmer for 1 minute, then return the fish and tofu to the wok. Cover and cook for 1 minute more, until the fish is cooked through. Serve immediately, sprinkled with spring onion.

COOK'S TIP For an extra crunchy texture you can add a handful of mangetouts (snow peas) or 30ml/2 tbsp shredded cooked bamboo shoots when you return the fish and tofu to the wok in step 4.

SERVES 4

600g/1lb 6oz monkfish or cod fillet, or any firm-fleshed fish, membrane or skin removed
75ml/5 tbsp vegetable oil
200g/7oz firm tofu, drained and cut into bitesize cubes
2 garlic cloves, crushed
15ml/1 tbsp yellow bean sauce
15ml/1 tbsp dark soy sauce
3 fresh red chillies, seeded and finely chopped
5ml/1 tsp caster (superfine) sugar
1 chopped spring onion (scallion), to garnish

Braised duck with tofu

SERVES 6–8

2 duck breast fillets
75ml/5 tbsp groundnut
(peanut) oil
250g/9oz firm tofu, drained
and cut into bitesize cubes
25oz/1 oz fresh root ginger,
finely grated
4 garlic cloves, crushed
1 large onion, sliced
30ml/2 tbsp hoisin sauce
15ml/1 tbsp oyster sauce
30ml/2 tbsp Chinese wine or
dry sherry
pickled ginger

As a winter warmer this dish is very comforting, with its wine sauce and blended seasonings that bring out the flavour of the duck. While fruity sauces like plum really cut the fat of duck, aromatics like garlic and ginger also do the same job. Tofu pieces with their firm outside and soft centre provide the perfect contrast.

1 Cut the duck breasts into slices about 5mm/¼in thick.

2 Heat the oil in a wok until smoking hot and fry the tofu cubes until a brown skin forms on all sides. Remove with a slotted spoon and drain on kitchen paper. Set aside. Add the duck pieces to the wok and fry in the remaining oil over a high heat for 2 minutes. Remove with a slotted spoon and drain on kitchen paper.

3 Pour out all but 15ml/1 tbsp of the oil and fry the ginger, garlic and onion for 1 minute, or until nearly brown. Add the hoisin sauce, oyster sauce, wine or sherry and 600ml/1 pint/2½ cups water, then bring to the boil.

4 Return the duck to the wok and braise over a high heat for 2 minutes, or until the sauce is thick and glossy. Add the tofu and cook for a further 3 minutes. Serve with slices of pickled ginger to taste. These come in thin slices in jars or vacuum-packed.

DESSERTS

At first sight these scrumptious desserts look really self-indulgent, but they are far from being packed with calories and cream. There are clever tofu versions of everyone's favourites, from Chocolate Mousse to Strawberry and Vanilla Tofu Ice – perfect for family meals and special enough for guests.

SERVES 6

2 large ripe mangoes
200ml/7fl oz/scant 1 cup
coconut cream
200g/7oz silken tofu
45ml/3 tbsp maple syrup
mint sprigs and thin slices of
lime rind, to decorate

Mango and coconut tofu whip

This deliciously smooth dessert has a truly tropical taste. The slightly resinous flavour of mango is superbly complemented by coconut cream. Add the magical texture of silken tofu and you have perfection in a glass.

1 Using a sharp knife, peel and stone (pit) the mangoes and coarsely chop the flesh. Place the flesh in a blender or food processor with the coconut cream and silken tofu.

2 Add the maple syrup and process to a smooth, rich cream. Pour into serving glasses or bowls and chill for at least 1 hour in before serving. Decorate with mint sprigs and some thinly sliced lime rind.

Berry and tofu smoothie

This energizing blend is simply bursting with goodness, just what you need when the morning has got off to a slow start. Not only is tofu a perfect source of protein, it is also rich in minerals and contains nutrients that protect against disease.

1 Roughly chop the tofu, then hull and roughly chop the strawberries. Reserve a few strawberry chunks.

2 Put all the ingredients in a blender or food processor and blend until completely smooth, scraping the mixture down from the side of the bowl, if necessary.

3 Pour into tumblers and sprinkle with extra seeds and strawberry chunks.

MAKES 2 GLASSES

250g/9oz firm tofu, drained
200g/7oz/1¾ cups
strawberries
45ml/3 tbsp pumpkin or
sunflower seeds, plus extra for
sprinkling
30–45ml/2–3 tbsp clear honey
juice of 2 large oranges
juice of 1 lemon

Date and tofu ice

This creamy date and apple ice cream is generously spiced with cinnamon and not only does it taste good but is also packed with soya protein, contains no added sugar, is low in fat and free from all dairy products.

1 Put the dates in a pan. Pour in 300ml/½ pint/1¼ cups of the apple juice and leave to soak for 4 hours. Simmer for 10 minutes, then leave to cool. Using a slotted spoon, lift out one-quarter of the dates, chop coarsely and set aside.

2 Put the remaining dates in a food processor or blender and process to a purée. Add the cinnamon and process with enough of the remaining apple juice to make a smooth paste.

3 Add the cubes of tofu, a few at a time, processing after each addition. Finally, add the remaining apple juice and the soya milk.

4 By hand: Pour the mixture into a plastic tub or similar freezerproof container and freeze for 4 hours, beating once with a fork, electric mixer or in a food processor to break up the ice crystals. After this time, beat well again with a fork to make sure that the texture is completely smooth.
Using an ice cream maker: Churn the mixture until very thick, but not thick enough to scoop. Scrape into a plastic tub with a lid.

5 Stir in some of the chopped dates and freeze for 2–3 hours, until firm.

6 Place scoops of the ice in four dessert glasses and decorate with the remaining chopped dates before serving.

COOK'S TIP As tofu is a non–dairy product it will not blend completely, so don't be concerned if the mixture contains tiny flecks of tofu.

SERVES 4

250g/9oz/1½ cups stoned (pitted) dates
600ml/1 pint/2½ cups apple juice
5ml/1 tsp ground cinnamon
300g/11oz firm tofu, drained and cut into bitesize cubes
150ml/¼ pint/⅔ cup unsweetened soya milk

SERVES 8

450ml/¾ pint/scant 2 cups
soya milk
50g/2oz/¼ cup caster
(superfine) sugar
20ml/4 tsp cornflour
(cornstarch)
5ml/1 tsp vanilla essence
(extract) or 1 vanilla pod (bean)
500g/1¼lb silken tofu
15ml/1 tbsp sunflower oil
30ml/2 tbsp maple syrup
250g/9oz/2 cups strawberries,
hulled and halved, plus extra
to decorate

Strawberry and vanilla tofu ice

This pretty pink dairy-free ice has a remarkably creamy taste,
largely due to the smooth silken tofu. Serve with slices of
fresh strawberry, or in a cone, drizzled with strawberry syrup.

1 Reserve 60ml/4 tbsp soya milk, then pour the remainder into a
large pan and bring to the boil over a medium heat. Blend
the sugar and cornflour with the reserved milk in a bowl. Add the
sugar mixture and vanilla essence or vanilla pod to the warm milk.
Simmer, stirring constantly, for 2 minutes, until thickened.

2 When the mixture is thick enough to coat the back of the
spoon, pour it into a bowl. Remove and discard the vanilla pod.
Cover the surface with a sheet of greaseproof or waxed paper to
prevent a skin forming, then leave to cool.

3 Process the tofu, oil, maple syrup and strawberries in a food
processor or blender until smooth and creamy.

4 Mix the strawberry mixture into the vanilla custard, pour into a
freezerproof container and freeze for 2 hours. Whisk the half-
frozen mixture until smooth, then return to the freezer for 1 hour.
Whisk again and freeze until solid. Remove the ice from the
freezer 20 minutes before serving to soften.

Chocolate tofu mousse

SERVES 6-8

60ml/4 tbsp golden (light corn) syrup
115g/4oz plain (semisweet) chocolate (preferably 70% cocoa solids), broken into pieces
15ml/1 tbsp instant coffee mixed with 30ml/2 tbsp boiling water or 30ml/2 tbsp very strong brewed coffee (optional)
350g/12oz silken tofu
2 eggs, separated
natural (plain) yogurt, to serve
cocoa powder (unsweetened), to decorate

All the flavour of a traditional mousse, but the addition of tofu means far less fat. If making for children, omit the coffee and stir grated orange rind into the melted chocolate.

1 Place the syrup, chocolate and coffee, if using, in a heatproof bowl set over a pan of simmering water until melted. Stir together, remove from the heat then leave to cool slightly.

2 Place the tofu and chocolate mixture in a food processor or blender and process for 1–2 minutes. Add the egg yolks and process to a thick cream. Transfer to a large bowl.

3 Whisk the egg whites in a clean, grease-free bowl until stiff, then gradually fold into the chocolate mixture, a little at a time, using a rubber spatula.

4 Spoon the mousse into serving glasses, pots or cups and chill in the refrigerator until set. Spoon a little yogurt on top of each mousse, sprinkle with cocoa powder, and serve.

Tofu berry cheesecake

A glorious fake, this cheesecake does not contain cheese, but no one will be able to tell. Instead, it owes its wonderful texture to a mixture of tofu and yogurt.

1 To make the base, place the low-fat spread or margarine and apple juice in a pan and heat them gently until the spread or margarine has melted. Crush the bran flakes and stir them into the apple juice mixture.

2 Tip the mixture into a 23cm/9in loose-based round flan tin or pie pan and press down firmly with your fingers. Leave the base to cool, then chill until set.

3 To make the filling, place the tofu and yogurt in a food processor and process them until smooth. Soak the gelatine in the apple juice, then heat to dissolve. Stir into the tofu mixture.

4 Spread the tofu mixture over the base, smoothing it evenly. Chill for 1–2 hours, until the filling has set.

5 Carefully remove the flan tin and place the cheesecake on a serving plate.

6 Arrange the soft fruit on top of the cheesecake. Place the redcurrant jelly in a small bowl and add the hot water. Stir well until the jelly has melted. Leave it to cool and then spoon or lightly brush it over the fruit to serve.

COOK'S TIPS If the apple juice and bran flakes mixture sticks to your fingers and keeps coming away from the tin while you are trying to press it flat, try using the base of a clean jar instead.
• Use the same jar to remove the cake from the tin. Stand the base on the inverted jar and carefully slide off the ring part of the tin downwards.

SERVES 6

425g/15oz firm tofu, drained
300g/11oz sheep's milk yogurt
25ml/1½ tbsp/1½ sachets powdered gelatine
90ml/6 tbsp apple juice
175g/6oz/1¾ cups soft fruit, such as raspberries, strawberries, redcurrants and blueberries
30ml/2 tbsp redcurrant jelly
30ml/2 tbsp hot water

For the base
50g/2oz/¼ cup dairy-free, low-fat spread or margarine
30ml/2 tbsp apple juice
115g/4oz/6 cups bran flakes

Peach and tofu melba

SERVES 4

4 peaches
30ml/2 tbsp caster (superfine)
sugar
2 vanilla pods (beans)
raspberries, to decorate
60ml/4 tbsp soya yogurt, to
serve

For the vanilla sauce
700g/1lb 6oz silken tofu
50g/2oz/½ cup icing
(confectioners') sugar
105ml/7 tbsp apple juice
2 drops vanilla essence
(extract)

For the raspberry sauce
300g/11oz/scant 2 cups fresh
or frozen raspberries

The use of silken tofu means this delicious dish retains the richness of cream but without the fat. Peach Melba has become one of the world's favourite desserts and is the inspiration for this fabulous dairy-free version. You do need to use fresh as opposed to canned peaches, as they lift it to a very special dish.

1 Place four wide, individual serving glasses in the freezer to chill. Meanwhile place the whole peaches in a pan and add just enough water to cover. Add the sugar and the vanilla pods. Bring to the boil, lower the heat and simmer gently for 10 minutes. Remove the peaches from the pan with a slotted spoon and set aside.

2 Leave the peaches until they are cool enough to handle, then carefully peel off the skins with your fingers. If the skins do not come off easily, put the peaches back in the water and simmer for a further 2 minutes.

3 Cut the peaches in half and gently ease out the stone (pit). Set aside while you make the sauces.

4 To make the vanilla sauce, put the tofu with the icing sugar in a food processor or blender and add the apple juice and vanilla essence. Process until smooth, then tip into a bowl and set aside in the refrigerator until required.

5 To make the raspberry sauce, put all but four of the raspberries in a food processor or blender and process until puréed. If you don't like the pips (seeds), then push the purée through a sieve with a spatula.

6 Remove the glasses from the freezer and place two peach halves in the base of each glass, followed by some of the vanilla sauce. Drizzle over some of the raspberry sauce. Add a spoonful of soya yogurt and decorate with the reserved fresh raspberries before serving.

SERVES 6

15g/½oz/1 tbsp cornflour
(cornstarch)
25g/1oz/2 tbsp demerara (raw)
sugar
175ml/6fl oz/¾ cup soya milk
175g/6oz silken tofu
2.5ml/½ tsp vanilla essence
(extract)
2 large ripe bananas
18cm/7in pre-baked pastry
case (pie shell)
75g/3oz/¾ cup pecan nut
halves
7.5ml/½ tbsp maple syrup or
clear honey, to glaze

Banana and pecan tofu pie

This variation of a classic American dessert is guaranteed to
become a firm family favourite. The combination of crisp
pastry, creamy vanilla-tofu custard, sweet banana and crunchy
pecans glazed with maple syrup is absolutely irresistible.

1 Put the cornflour and sugar in a pan and stir together. Add a
little of the milk and combine into a smooth paste. Add the rest
of the milk gradually, stirring between each addition.

2 Place the pan over a low heat and cook, stirring constantly,
until the custard thickens, coating the back of the spoon.

3 Place the custard, tofu, vanilla essence and 1 banana in a
blender or food processor and blend until smooth.

4 Slice the remaining bananas and arrange the slices over the
base of the pre-baked pastry case. Spoon the tofu mixture on top
and spread evenly. Decorate with the pecan nuts then glaze with
the maple syrup. Chill the tart for 1 hour before serving.

350g/12oz firm tofu, drained
and thinly sliced
juice and grated rind of 1 lime
30ml/2 tbsp coconut oil
60ml/4 tbsp maple syrup
8 fresh or frozen strawberries,
hulled
8 small soft corn taco shells

Sweet tofu tacos

Tacos are the ultimate savoury Mexican finger food, but here
they are served as a sweet vegan treat, still eaten hot but
made with slices of tofu, fresh fruit and soft taco shells.

1 Arrange the tofu slices in a shallow dish. Pour over the lime
juice and rind and set aside to marinate for half an hour.

2 When you're ready to prepare the tacos, heat the oil in a small
pan over a medium heat. Add the marinated tofu, lime, maple
syrup and the strawberries and cook, stirring regularly, until soft
and piping hot.

3 Heat the tortillas one by one in a dry frying pan for about 30
seconds on each side until hot. Keep hot by putting them inside a
clean dish towel when each one is ready.

4 To assemble, stack two tacos on each serving plate, then spoon
an equal amount of the tofu and strawberry mixture on to each.
Pour any remaining syrup from the pan over the warm tacos.
Serve immediately.

Carrot cake with silken tofu frosting

SERVES 8

90g/3½oz/7 tbsp margarine
5ml/1 tsp cardamom pods
225g/8oz/2 cups wholemeal
(whole-wheat) or plain (all-
purpose) flour
15ml/1 tbsp baking powder
130g/4½oz/⅔ cup demerara
(raw) sugar
225g/8oz carrots, coarsely
grated
50g/2oz/scant ½ cup sultanas
(golden raisins)
5ml/1 tsp ground cinnamon
pinch of ground cloves
75ml/5 tbsp sunflower oil
2 eggs, lightly beaten

For the frosting
175g/6oz silken tofu
25g/1oz/¼ cup icing
(confectioners') sugar
7.5ml/½ tbsp apple juice
drop of vanilla essence
(extract)
finely grated rind of ½ orange

Everybody loves this sweet, moist cake with its delicious creamy tofu frosting. It makes a great dessert for family meals and when entertaining, and is also a tasty pick-me-up when you need a mid-morning coffee break – in the unlikely event of any being left over.

1 Preheat the oven to 160°C/325°F/Gas 3. Grease and line an 18cm/7in loose-based cake tin or pan.

2 Melt the margarine in a small pan over a low heat, then leave to cool.

3 Remove the seeds from the cardamom pods, discarding the pods. Place the seeds in a mortar and crush with a pestle.

4 Mix the flour, baking powder, sugar, carrots, sultanas and the spices together in a large bowl.

5 Add the margarine, oil and eggs and mix to a soft cake batter.

6 Spoon or pour the mixture into the prepared cake tin and smooth the top. Bake for 60–65 minutes, or until a skewer inserted into the centre comes out clean and the top is golden brown and firm to the touch.

7 Remove the cake from the oven and place, still in the tin, on a wire rack to cool completely. Carefully remove the cake from the tin and return to the wire rack for frosting.

8 Meanwhile, make the frosting by placing the tofu and icing sugar in a food processor or blender. Add the apple juice, vanilla and orange rind. Process the mixture until smooth and creamy. Spoon the frosting over the top of the cake and spread with the back of a knife or spatula.

Nutritional notes

The nutritional analysis given for each recipe is calculated per portion (i.e. serving or item), unless otherwise stated. If the recipe gives a range, such as Serves 4–6, then the nutritional analysis will be for the smaller portion size, i.e. 6 servings. The analysis does not include optional ingredients, such as salt added to taste.

Hot-and-sweet vegetable and tofu soup : Energy 103kcal/434kJ; Protein 5.5g; Carbohydrate 13.3g, of which sugars 12.8g; Fat 3.5g, of which saturates 0.4g; Cholesterol 0mg; Calcium 320mg; Fibre 0.7g; Sodium 769mg.

Vegetable and marinated fried tofu: Energy 319kcal/1327kJ; Protein 23.1g; Carbohydrate 17g, of which sugars 14.7g; Fat 18g, of which saturates 0.8g; Cholesterol 0mg; Calcium 1231mg; Fibre 10.3g; Sodium 79mg.

Miso broth with spring onions and tofu: Energy 71kcal/297kJ; Protein 7.2g; Carbohydrate 4.2g, of which sugars 3.5g; Fat 2.9g, of which saturates 0.4g; Cholesterol 0mg; Calcium 372mg; Fibre 2.6g; Sodium 884mg.

Tofu and bean sprout soup with rice noodles: Energy 265kcal/1105kJ; Protein 10.3g; Carbohydrate 36.6g, of which sugars 4.6g; Fat 8.2g, of which saturates 1.4g; Cholesterol 0mg; Calcium 298mg; Fibre 1.3g; Sodium 279mg.

Potato wedges with tofu dip: Energy 320kcal/1340kJ; Protein 8.2g; Carbohydrate 38.5g, of which sugars 3.1g; Fat 15.9g, of which saturates 2.3g; Cholesterol 0mg; Calcium 246mg; Fibre 2.3g; Sodium 28mg.

Tom yam gung with tofu: Energy 121kcal/504kJ; Protein 7.1g; Carbohydrate 3.5g, of which sugars 3g; Fat 8.9g, of which saturates 1.1g; Cholesterol 0mg; Calcium 406mg; Fibre 1g; Sodium 808mg.

Spicy soft tofu and seafood stew: Energy 170kcal/709kJ; Protein 21.4g; Carbohydrate 2.1g, of which sugars 1.5g; Fat 8.4g, of which saturates 1.5g; Cholesterol 140mg; Calcium 378mg; Fibre 0.8g; Sodium 734mg.

Tofu spring rolls: Energy 175kcal/730kJ; Protein 9.5g; Carbohydrate 12g, of which sugars 2.2g; Fat 10.2g, of which saturates 1.7g; Cholesterol 49mg; Calcium 96mg; Fibre 1.2g; Sodium 686mg.

Deep-fried fish and tofu cakes: Energy 270kcal/1123kJ; Protein 21g; Carbohydrate 18g, of which sugars 1g; Fat 17g, of which saturates 2g; Cholesterol 98mg; Calcium 178mg; Fibre 0g; Sodium 257mg.

Sushi rice in tofu bags: Energy 528kcal/2195kJ; Protein 31.2g; Carbohydrate 8.7g, of which sugars 6.8g; Fat 35.1g, of which saturates 3.1g; Cholesterol 0mg; Calcium 1696mg; Fibre 3.2g; Sodium 5007mg.

Deep-fried tofu balls: Energy 40kcal/164kJ; Protein 3.9g; Carbohydrate 1.1g, of which sugars 0.9g; Fat 2.2g, of which saturates 0.4g; Cholesterol 24mg; Calcium 187mg; Fibre 0.3g; Sodium 380mg.

Tofu falafel with hummus: Energy 484kcal/2024kJ; Protein 23g; Carbohydrate 36g, of which sugars 6g; Fat 28g, of which saturates 5g; Cholesterol 69mg; Calcium 288mg; Fibre 5g; Sodium 93mg.

Tofu and seafood wontons: Energy 451kcal/874kJ; Protein 30g; Carbohydrate 13g, of which sugars 1g; Fat 31g, of which saturates 4g; Cholesterol 225mg; Calcium 207mg; Fibre 1g; Sodium 762mg.

Thai tempeh cakes with dipping sauce: Energy 79kcal/332kJ; Protein 4.5g; Carbohydrate 9.1g, of which sugars 4.3g; Fat 2.3g, of which saturates 0.4g; Cholesterol 26mg; Calcium 192mg; Fibre 0.8g; Sodium 15mg.

Pan-fried tofu with caramelized sauce: Energy 291kcal/1213kJ; Protein 23g; Carbohydrate 7.8g, of which sugars 1.3g; Fat 19.1g, of which saturates 3.4g; Cholesterol 209mg; Calcium 1014mg; Fibre 0.8g; Sodium 88mg.

Stuffed pan-fried tofu: Energy 291kcal/1213kJ; Protein 23g; Carbohydrate 7.8g, of which sugars 1.3g; Fat 19.1g, of which saturates 3.4g; Cholesterol 209mg; Calcium 1014mg; Fibre 0.8g; Sodium 88mg.

Tofu, broccoli and mushroom salad: Energy 148kcal/6141kJ; Protein 9g; Carbohydrate 4g, of which sugars 3g; Fat 11g, of which saturates 1g; Cholesterol 0mg; Calcium 248mg; Fibre 1.5g; Sodium 1077mg.

Chicory and avocado salad with tofu-dill dressing: Energy 453kcal/1871kJ; Protein 12.6g; Carbohydrate 6.7g, of which sugars 3.6g; Fat 42.5g, of which saturates 6.5g; Cholesterol 0mg; Calcium 513mg; Fibre 5.7g; Sodium 117mg.

Green bean and tomato salad with tofu pesto: Energy 383kcal/1581kJ; Protein 9.4g; Carbohydrate 9.6g, of which sugars 7.8g; Fat 34.4g, of which saturates 4.6g; Cholesterol 0mg; Calcium 284mg; Fibre 6g; Sodium 14mg.

Spiralized vegetable salad with tofu dressing: Energy 262kcal/1093kJ; Protein 17.8g; Carbohydrate 20.3g, of which sugars 12.4g; Fat 13.6g, of which saturates 1g; Cholesterol 171mg; Fibre 4.2g; Sodium 22mg.

Stir-fried crispy tofu: Energy 510kcal/2122kJ; Protein 33.5g; Carbohydrate 18.8g, of which sugars 17.2g; Fat 33.9g, of which saturates 2.2g; Cholesterol 0mg; Calcium 1893mg; Fibre 2.2g; Sodium 1085mg.

Stir-fried tofu with Chinese chive stems: Energy 167kcal/690kJ; Protein 7g; Carbohydrate 3g, of which sugars 3g; Fat 14g, of which saturates 2g; Cholesterol 0mg; Calcium 353mg; Fibre 2.1g; Sodium 542mg.

Roasted peppers with tofu: Energy 100kcal/417kJ; Protein 5.5g; Carbohydrate 12g, of which sugars 11.3g; Fat 3.6g, of which saturates 0.8g; Cholesterol 55mg; Calcium 29mg; Fibre 3.9g; Sodium 388mg.

Snake beans with tofu: Energy 263kcal/1091kJ; Protein 14.5g; Carbohydrate 13.3g, of which sugars 10g; Fat 17.2g, of which saturates 3g; Cholesterol 0mg; Calcium 335mg; Fibre 4.7g; Sodium 1353mg.

Fried garlic tofu: Energy 198kcal/819kJ; Protein 12g; Carbohydrate 2g, of which sugars 2g; Fat.16g, of which saturates 7g; Cholesterol 27mg; Calcium 645mg; Fibre 2g; Sodium 884mg.

Marinated tofu and broccoli with crispy fried shallots: Energy 202kcal/840kJ; Protein 16.5g; Carbohydrate 6.9g, of which sugars 5.6g; Fat 12.1g, of which saturates 1.7g; Cholesterol 0mg; Calcium 750mg; Fibre 3.5g; Sodium 938mg.

Steamed egg custard: Energy 177kcal/735kJ; Protein 14g; Carbohydrate 1g, of which sugars 1g; Fat 13g of which saturates 3g; Cholesterol 232mg; Calcium 391mg; Fibre 0g; Sodium 267mg.saturates 3g; Cholesterol 232mg; Calcium 391mg; Fibre 0g; Sodium 267mg.

Peanut and tofu cutlets: Energy 485kcal/2021kJ; Protein 19.7g; Carbohydrate 25.6g, of which sugars 4.1g; Fat 34.5g, of which saturates 5.9g; Cholesterol 0mg; Calcium 352mg; Fibre 0.6g; Sodium 538mg.

Vegetable tofu burgers: Energy 412kcal/1713kJ; Protein 14g; Carbohydrate 57g, of which sugars 7g; Fat.16g, of which saturates 2g; Cholesterol 0mg; Calcium 400mg; Fibre 8g; Sodium 788mg.

Tofu tortillas: Energy 442kcal/1865kJ; Protein 17.4g; Carbohydrate 75.6g, of which sugars 7.4g; Fat 9.7g, of which saturates 1.4g; Cholesterol 0mg; Calcium 478mg; Fibre 9.8g; Sodium 811mg.

Fried tofu and rice noodles: Energy 392kcal/1631kJ; Protein 12g; Carbohydrate 43.6g, of which sugars 2.4g; Fat 18.2g, of which saturates 2.9g; Cholesterol 0mg; Calcium 536mg; Fibre 2.2g; Sodium 285mg.

Tofu and pepper kebabs: Energy 187kcal/778kJ; Protein 10.2g; Carbohydrate 16.8g, of which sugars 15.1g; Fat 9.1g, of which saturates 1.6g; Cholesterol 0mg; Calcium 342mg; Fibre 3.7g; Sodium 214mg.

Tofu stir-fry with peanut sauce: Energy 252Kcal/1045kJ; Protein 10g; Carbohydrate 12g, of which sugars 8.5g; Fat 18g, of which saturates 3g; Cholesterol 0mg; Calcium 319mg; Fibre 3.6g; Sodium 1055mg.

Sweet-and-sour vegetables with tofu: Energy 177kcal/736kJ; Protein 10.5g; Carbohydrate 13.7g, of which sugars 12.5g; Fat 9.2g, of which saturates 1.5g; Cholesterol 0mg; Calcium 461mg; Fibre 4.3g; Sodium 844mg.

Braised tofu: Energy 118kcal/490kJ; Protein 8.2g; Carbohydrate 14g, of which sugars 8.8g; Fat 3.7g, of which saturates 0.4g; Cholesterol 0mg; Calcium 385mg; Fibre 1.9g; Sodium 1076mg.

Salad wraps with pumpkin, tofu, peanuts and basil: Energy 402Kcal/1669kJ; Protein 14g; Carbohydrate 29g, of which sugars 13g; Fat 26g, of which saturates 5g; Cholesterol 0mg; Calcium 321mg; Fibre 4.1g; Sodium 0.4g.

Vegetable and tofu cake with mustard dip: Energy 320kcal/1334kJ; Protein 23g; Carbohydrate 16.4g, of which sugars 14.9g; Fat 18.7g, of which saturates 3.7g; Cholesterol 285mg; Calcium 662mg; Fibre 3.8g; Sodium 657mg.

Spicy tofu with lemon grass, basil and peanuts: Energy 120Kcal/500kJ; Protein 3g; Carbohydrate 5g, of which sugars 3g; Fat 10g, of which saturates 2g; Cholesterol 0mg; Calcium 36mg; Fibre 3.3g; Sodium 0.2g.

Spiced tofu stir-fry: Energy 242kcal/1004kJ; Protein 11g; Carbohydrate 11.2g, of which sugars 8.9g; Fat 17.3g, of which saturates 2.9g; Cholesterol 0mg; Calcium 356mg; Fibre 3.4g; Sodium 1072mg.

Mushrooms with bean curd skins: Energy 33kcal/140kJ; Protein 3g; Carbohydrate 3g, of which sugars 1g; Fat 1g, of which saturates 0g; Cholesterol 0mg; Calcium 70g: Fibre2g; Sodium 252mg.

Crisp fried tofu in a tangy tomato sauce: Energy 234Kcal/974kJ; Protein 11g; Carbohydrate 11g, of which sugars 10.1g; Fat 16g, of which saturates 2g; Cholesterol 0mg; Calcium 619mg; Fibre 2.7g; Sodium 25mg.

Tofu and green bean curry: Energy 110kcal/460kJ; Protein 5.7g; Carbohydrate 10.2g, of which sugars 9.6g; Fat 5.5g, of which saturates 0.9g; Cholesterol 0mg; Calcium 282mg; Fibre 1.3g; Sodium 437mg.

Pock-marked tofu: Energy 276kcal/1143kJ; Protein 14g; Carbohydrate 6g, of which sugars 3g; Fat 22g, of which saturates 3g; Cholesterol 0mg; Calcium 837mg; Fibre 1g; Sodium 365mg.

Tofu with preserved bean curd: Energy 187kcal/779kJ; Protein 9g; Carbohydrate 10g, of which sugars 8g; Fat 12g, of which saturates 1g; Cholesterol 0mg; Calcium 376g: Fibre 5g; Sodium 12mg.

Braised tofu with mushrooms: Energy 152kcal/629kJ; Protein 8g; Carbohydrate 3g, of which sugars 1g; Fat 11g, of which saturates 1g; Cholesterol 0mg; Calcium 458mg; Fibre 1g; Sodium 323mg.

Potato rosti and tofu with fresh tomato and ginger sauce: Energy 453kcal/1897kJ; Protein 16g; Carbohydrate 47g, of which sugars 8g; Fat 24g, of which saturates 3g; Cholesterol 0mg; Calcium 609mg; Fibre 5g; Sodium 596mg.

Twice-cooked tempeh: Energy 486kcal/2032kJ; Protein 34.9g; Carbohydrate 31.5g, of which sugars 23.4g; Fat 27.4g, of which saturates 7.3g; Cholesterol 28mg; Calcium 502mg; Fibre 9.6g; Sodium 816mg.

Vegetable moussaka with tofu topping: Energy 768kcal/3255kJ; Protein 60.2g; Carbohydrate 109.6g, of which sugars 10.3g; Fat 13.1g, of which saturates 2.9g; Cholesterol 99mg; Calcium 357mg; Fibre 21.8g; Sodium 320mg.

Tofu and vegetable Thai curry: Energy 210kcal/873kJ; Protein 11g; Carbohydrate 15.1g, of which sugars 13.3g; Fat 12g, of which saturates 1.8g; Cholesterol 0mg; Calcium 328mg; Fibre 5g; Sodium 927mg.

Nasi goreng: Energy 463kcal/1929kJ; Protein 27.3g; Carbohydrate 49.4g, of which sugars 2.1g; Fat 17.1g, of which saturates 2.7g; Cholesterol 151mg; Calcium 49mg; Fibre 0.5g; Sodium 288mg.

Malaysian tofu and quinoa laksa: Energy 266kcal/1121kJ; Protein 12g; Carbohydrate 38g, of which sugars 12g; Fat 8g, of which saturates 1g; Cholesterol 0mg; Calcium 264mg; Fibre 4g; Sodium 152mg.

Tofu and wild rice: Energy 283kcal/1181kJ; Protein 9.5g; Carbohydrate 47.5g, of which sugars 2.3g; Fat 5.8g, of which saturates 0.7g; Cholesterol 0mg; Calcium 350mg; Fibre 0.7g; Sodium 6mg.

Noodles and rice with tofu and beansprout broth: Energy 690kcal/2900kJ; Protein 32.6g; Carbohydrate 97g, of which sugars 5.9g; Fat 20.7g, of which saturates 3.6g; Cholesterol 171mg; Calcium 328mg; Fibre 4.2g; Sodium 833mg.

Tofu with spiralized mooli noodles: Energy 474kcal/1983kJ;

Protein 49.7g; Carbohydrate 27.6g, of which sugars 5.3g; Fat 21.6g, of which saturates 1.9g; Cholesterol 231mg; Calcium 386mg; Fibre 0.3g; Sodium 670mg.

Teriyaki soba noodles with tofu and asparagus: Energy 519kcal/2162kJ; Protein 13g; Carbohydrate 77g, of which sugars 5g; Fat 16g, of which saturates 3g; Cholesterol 0mg; Calcium 397mg; Fibre 2g; Sodium 1093mg.

Indian mee goreng: Energy 478kcal/2010kJ; Protein 16.8g; Carbohydrate 64.2g, of which sugars 5.1g; Fat 18.9g, of which saturates 3.2g; Cholesterol 86mg; Calcium 323mg; Fibre 2.9g; Sodium 466mg.

Crispy fried tempeh and noodles: Energy 258kcal/1071kJ; Protein 14.8g; Carbohydrate 7.7g, of which sugars 5.5g; Fat 18.9g, of which saturates 2.6g; Cholesterol 0mg; Calcium 682mg; Fibre 1.7g; Sodium 2680mg.

Rice noodles with bean curd skins: Energy 417kcal/1713kJ; Protein 8g; Carbohydrate 5g, of which sugars 2g; Fat 20g, of which saturates 3g; Cholesterol 0mg; Calcium 113g: Fibre 3g; Sodium 521mg.

Vegetable and marinated tofu pasta: Energy 807kcal/3380kJ; Protein 42g; Carbohydrate 75g, of which sugars 21g; Fat.39g, of which saturates 3g; Cholesterol 0mg; Calcium 1987mg; Fibre 8g; Sodium 595mg.

Tofu balls with spaghetti: Energy 611kcal/2572kJ; Protein 23.7g; Carbohydrate 87.4g, of which sugars 19.4g; Fat 21.1g, of which saturates 2.5g; Cholesterol 0mg; Calcium 450mg; Fibre 10.4g; Sodium 323mg.

Soya bean paste stew: Energy 166kcal/690kJ; Protein 13g; Carbohydrate 4.8g, of which sugars 3.2g; Fat 10.7g, of which saturates 2.2g; Cholesterol 15mg; Calcium 169mg; Fibre 3.1g; Sodium 25mg.

Tofu and minced pork soup: Energy 244kcal/1014kJ; Protein 23g; Carbohydrate 2g, of which sugars 0g; Fat 16g, of which saturates 3g; Cholesterol 155mg; Calcium 345mg; Fibre 1g; Sodium 448mg.

Pork and tofu croquettes: Energy 256kcal/1063kJ; Protein 16.9g; Carbohydrate 6.5g, of which sugars 0.5g; Fat 18.2g, of which saturates 3.6g; Cholesterol 140mg; Calcium 351mg; Fibre 0.3g; Sodium 143mg.

Thai curry with chicken and tofu: Energy 354kcal/1484kJ; Protein 44.7g; Carbohydrate 12.9g, of which sugars 10.4g; Fat 14.1g, of which saturates 1.4g; Cholesterol 105mg; Calcium 495mg; Fibre 1.9g; Sodium 1132mg.

Tofu laksa: Energy 266 kcal/1121 kJ; Protein 12g; Carbohydrate 38g, of which sugars 12g; Fat 8g, of which saturates 1g; Cholesterol 0 mg; Calcium 264mg; Fibre 4g; Sodium 152 mg.

Mongolian seafood and tofu steamboat: Energy 163kcal/687kJ; Protein 29g; Carbohydrate 3g, of which sugars 1g; Fat 4g, of which saturates 1g; Cholesterol 172mg; Calcium 200mg; Fibre 1g; Sodium 581mg.

Braised tofu with crab: Energy 472kcal/1966kJ; Protein 46g; Carbohydrate 4g, of which sugars 2g; Fat 30g, of which saturates 2g; Cholesterol 121mg; Calcium 1684g: Fibre 1g; Sodium 592mg.

Seafood and tofu paella: Energy 378kcal/1583kJ; Protein 22.1g; Carbohydrate 53.2g, of which sugars 8.8g; Fat 7.7g, of which saturates 1.2g; Cholesterol 127mg; Calcium 402mg; Fibre 5.4g; Sodium 77mg.

Tofu fish in a spicy sauce: Energy 340kcal/1418kJ; Protein 31g; Carbohydrate 6g, of which sugars 2g; Fat 22g, of which saturates 3g; Cholesterol 21mg; Calcium 280mg; Fibre 0.1g; Sodium 2189mg.

Braised duck with tofu: Energy 179kcal/743kJ; Protein 11g; Carbohydrate 4g, of which sugars 2g; Fat 13g, of which saturates 3g; Cholesterol 41mg; Calcium 174mg; Fibre 0.5g; Sodium 179mg.

Mango and coconut tofu whip: Energy 189kcal/788kJ; Protein 4.4g; Carbohydrate 14.3g, of which sugars 13.5g; Fat 13.1g, of which saturates 10.2g; Cholesterol 0mg; Calcium 185mg; Fibre 1.7g; Sodium 4mg.

Berry and tofu smoothie: Energy 310kcal/1296kJ; Protein 15.7g; Carbohydrate 26.9g, of which sugars 22.6g; Fat 16.1g, of which saturates 1.7g; Cholesterol 0mg; Calcium 684mg; Fibre 2.5g; Sodium 19mg.

Date and tofu ice: Energy 290kcal/1232kJ; Protein 9.1g; Carbohydrate 58.2g, of which sugars 57.9g; Fat 3.9g, of which saturates 0.5g; Cholesterol 0mg; Calcium 407mg; Fibre 2.5g; Sodium 24mg.

Strawberry and vanilla tofu ice: Energy 124kcal/521kJ; Protein 6.7g; Carbohydrate 14g, of which sugars 11g; Fat 5g, of which saturates 0.6g; Cholesterol 0mg; Calcium 336mg; Fibre 0.7g; Sodium 24mg.

Chocolate mousse: Energy 150kcal/629kJ; Protein 6.2g; Carbohydrate 15.4g, of which sugars 15.1g; Fat 7.5g, of which saturates 3.1g; Cholesterol 59mg; Calcium 238mg; Fibre 0.5g; Sodium 44mg.

Tofu berry cheesecake: Energy 250kcal/1048kJ; Protein 10.5g; Carbohydrate 23.2g, of which sugars 13.6g; Fat 13.5g, of which saturates 4g; Cholesterol 7mg; Calcium 453mg; Fibre 3.9g; Sodium 290mg.

Peach and tofu melba: Energy 235kcal/993kJ; Protein 15.4g; Carbohydrate 28.2g, of which sugars 27.5g; Fat 7.6g, of which saturates 1g; Cholesterol 0mg; Calcium 919mg; Fibre 2.5g; Sodium 11mg.

Banana and pecan tofu pie: Energy 309kcal/1291kJ; Protein 4.3g; Carbohydrate 32.8g, of which sugars 14g; Fat 18.7g, of which saturates 3.7g; Cholesterol 5mg; Calcium 44mg; Fibre 2.4g; Sodium 145mg.

Sweet tacos: Energy 307kcal/1279kJ; Protein 7.1g; Carbohydrate 28.7g, of which sugars 11g; Fat 18.1g, of which saturates 7.5g; Cholesterol 0mg; Calcium 448mg; Fibre 0.4g; Sodium 7mg.

Carrot cake with silken tofu frosting: Energy 375kcal/1570kJ; Protein 7.7g; Carbohydrate 45g, of which sugars 27.4g; Fat 19.5g, of which saturates 3.4g; Cholesterol 58mg; Calcium 148mg; Fibre 4.4g; Sodium 108mg.

Index